TEACH YOURSELF

NETWORKING

VISUALLY™

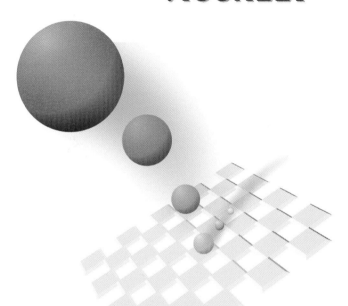

IDG's 3-D Visual™ Series

IDG BOOKS *From* **maranGraphics**™

IDG Books Worldwide, Inc.
An International Data Group Company
Foster City, CA • Indianapolis • Chicago • Southlake, TX

Teach Yourself Networking VISUALLY™

Published by
IDG Books Worldwide, Inc.
An International Data Group Company
919 E. Hillsdale Blvd., Suite 400
Foster City, CA 94404

Library of Congress Catalog Card No.: 97-080500

ISBN: 0-7645-6023-9

Printed in the United States of America

10 9 8 7 6 5 4 3 2

XX/XX/XX/XX/XX

Distributed in the United States by IDG Books Worldwide, Inc.

Distributed by Transworld Publishers Limited in the United Kingdom; by IDG Norge Books for Norway; by IDG Sweden Books for Sweden; by Woodslane Pty. Ltd. for Australia; by Woodslane Enterprises Ltd. for New Zealand; by Longman Singapore Publishers Ltd. for Singapore, Malaysia, Thailand, and Indonesia; by Simron Pty. Ltd. for South Africa; by Toppan Company Ltd. for Japan; by Distribuidora Cuspide for Argentina; by Livraria Cultura for Brazil; by Ediciencia S.A. for Ecuador; by Addison-Wesley Publishing Company for Korea; by Ediciones ZETA S.C.R. Ltda. for Peru; by WS Computer Publishing Corporation, Inc., for the Philippines; by Unalis Corporation for Taiwan; by Contemporanea de Ediciones for Venezuela; by Computer Book & Magazine Store for Puerto Rico; by Express Computer Distributors for the Caribbean and West Indies. Authorized Sales Agent: Anthony Rudkin Associates for the Middle East and North Africa.

For corporate orders, please call maranGraphics at 800-469-6616.

For general information on IDG Books Worldwide's books in the U.S., please call our Consumer Customer Service department at 800-762-2974.

For reseller information, including discounts and premium sales, please call our Reseller Customer Service department at 800-434-3422.

For information on where to purchase IDG Books Worldwide's books outside the U.S., please contact our International Sales department at 415-655-3200 or fax 415-655-3295.

For information on foreign language translations, please contact our Foreign & Subsidiary Rights department at 415-655-3021 or fax 415-655-3281.

For sales inquiries and special prices for bulk quantities, please contact our Sales department at 415-655-3200.

For information on using IDG Books Worldwide's books in the classroom or for ordering examination copies, please contact our Educational Sales department at 800-434-2086 or fax 817-251-8174.

For press review copies, author interviews, or other publicity information, please contact our Public Relations department at 415-655-3000 or fax 415-655-3299.

For authorization to photocopy items for corporate, personal, or educational use, please contact maranGraphics at 800-469-6616.

Trademark Acknowledgments

Permissions

U.S. Corporate Sales	U.S. Trade Sales
Contact maranGraphics at (800) 469-6616 or Fax (905) 890-9434.	Contact IDG Books at (800) 434-3422 or (415) 655-3000.

Welcome to the world of IDG Books Worldwide.

IDG Books Worldwide, Inc., is a subsidiary of International Data Group, the world's largest publisher of computer-related information and the leading global provider of information services on information technology. IDG was founded more than 25 years ago and now employs more than 8,500 people worldwide. IDG publishes more than 270 computer publications in over 75 countries (see listing below). More than 90 million people read one or more IDG publications each month.

Launched in 1990, IDG Books Worldwide is today the #1 publisher of best-selling computer books in the United States. We are proud to have received eight awards from the Computer Press Association in recognition of editorial excellence and three from Computer Currents' First Annual Readers' Choice Awards. Our best-selling ...For Dummies® series has more than 25 million copies in print with translations in 30 languages. IDG Books Worldwide, through a joint venture with IDG's Hi-Tech Beijing, became the first U.S. publisher to publish a computer book in the People's Republic of China. In record time, IDG Books Worldwide has become the first choice for millions of readers around the world who want to learn how to better manage their businesses.

Our mission is simple: Every one of our books is designed to bring extra value and skill-building instructions to the reader. Our books are written by experts who understand and care about our readers. The knowledge base of our editorial staff comes from years of experience in publishing, education, and journalism - experience which we use to produce books for the '90s. In short, we care about books, so we attract the best people. We devote special attention to details such as audience, interior design, use of icons, and illustrations. And because we use an efficient process of authoring, editing, and desktop publishing our books electronically, we can spend more time ensuring superior content and spend less time on the technicalities of making books.

You can count on our commitment to deliver high-quality books at competitive prices on topics you want to read about. At IDG Books Worldwide, we continue in the IDG tradition of delivering quality for more than 25 years. You'll find no better book on a subject than one from IDG Books Worldwide.

John Kilcullen
President and CEO
IDG Books Worldwide, Inc.

IDG Books Worldwide, Inc., is a subsidiary of International Data Group, the world's largest publisher of computer-related information and the leading global provider of information services on information technology. International Data Group publishes over 276 computer publications in over 75 countries. Ninety million people read one or more International Data Group publications each month. International Data Group's publications include: Argentina: Annuario de Informatica, Computerworld Argentina, PC World Argentina; Australia: Australian Macworld, Client/Server Journal, Computer Living, Computerworld, Computerworld 100, Digital News, IT Casebook, Network World, On-line World Australia, PC World, Publishing Essentials, Reseller, WebMaster; Austria: Computerwelt Österreich, Networks Austria, PC Tip; Belarus: PC World Belarus; Belgium: Data News; Brazil: Annuário de Informática, Computerworld Brazil, Connections, Super Game Power, Macworld, PC Player, PC World Brazil, Publish Brazil, Reseller News; Bulgaria: Computerworld Bulgaria, Networkworld/Bulgaria, PC & MacWorld Bulgaria; Canada: CIO Canada, Client/Server World, ComputerWorld Canada, InfoCanada, Network World Canada; Chile: Computerworld Chile, PC World Chile; Colombia: Computerworld Colombia, PC World Colombia; Costa Rica: PC World Centro America; The Czech and Slovak Republics: Computerworld Czechoslovakia, Elektronika Czechoslovakia, Macworld Czech Republic, PC World Czechoslovakia; Denmark: Communications World, Computerworld Danmark, Macworld Danmark, PC Privat Danmark, PC World Danmark, PC World Danmark Supplements, TECH World; Dominican Republic: PC World Republica Dominicana; Ecuador: PC World Ecuador; Egypt: Computerworld Middle East, PC World Middle East; El Salvador: PC World Centro America; Finland: MikroPC, Tietoverkko, Tietoviikko; France: Distributique, Golden, Hebdo-Distributique, Info PC, Le Guide du Monde Informatique, Le Monde Informatique, Reseaux & Telecoms; Germany: Computer Partner, Computerwoche, Computerwoche Extra, Computerwoche Focus, I/M Information Management, Macwelt, PC Welt; Greece: GamePro, Multimedia World; Guatemala: PC World Centro America; Honduras: PC World Centro America; Hong Kong: Computerworld Hong Kong, PCWorld Hong Kong, Publish in Asia; Hungary: ABCD CD-ROM, Computerworld Szamitastechnika, PC & Mac World Hungary, PC-X Magazine; Iceland: Tolvuheimur/PC World Island; India: Information Systems Computerworld, PC World India, Publish in Asia; Indonesia: InfoKomputer PC World, Komputek Computerworld, Publish in Asia; Ireland: ComputerScope, PC Live!; Israel: People & Computers; Italy: Computerworld Italia, Computerworld Italia Special Editions, Macworld Italia, Networking Italia, PC Shopping, PC World Italia, PC World/Walt Disney; Japan: DTP World, HP Open World Japan, Macworld Japan, Nikkei Personal Computing, Open World Japan, OS/2 World Japan, SunWorld Japan, Windows World Japan; Kenya: East African Computer News; Korea: Hi-Tech Information/Computerworld, Macworld Korea, PC World Korea; Macedonia: PC World Macedonia; Malaysia: Computerworld Malaysia, PC World Malaysia, Publish in Asia; Mexico: Computerworld Mexico, Macworld, PC World Mexico; Myanmar: PC World Myanmar; Netherlands: Computer! Totaal, LAN Magazine, LanWorld Buyers Guide, Macworld, Net Magazine, Totaal! Beurskrant; New Zealand: Absolute Beginner's Guide, Computer Buyer, Computer Industry Directory, Computerworld New Zealand, MTB, Network World, PC World New Zealand; Nicaragua: PC World Centro America; Nigeria: PC World Nigeria; Norway: Computerworld Norge, Computerworld Privat (Datamagasinet), CW Rapport Norge, IDG's KURSGUIDE, Macworld Norge, Multimediaworld, PC World Ekspress, PC World Nettverk, PC World Norge, PC World's Produktguide, Windows World Spesial; Pakistan: Computerworld Pakistan, PC World Pakistan; Panama: PC World Panama; P. R. of China: China Computer Users, China Computerworld, China Infoworld, China Telecom World Weekly, Computer & Communication, Electronic Design China, Electronics Today, Electronics Weekly, Game Camp, Game Soft, Network World China, PC World China, Popular Computer Weekly, Software Weekly, Software World, Telecom World; Peru: Computerworld Peru, PC World Profesional Peru, PC World Peru; Poland: Computerworld Poland, Computerworld Special Report, Macworld, Networld, PC World Komputer; Philippines: Computerworld Philippines, PC World Philippines, Publish in Asia; Portugal: Cerebro/PC World, Computerworld/Correio Informático, Dealer World Portugal, Mac*In/PC*In, Multimedia World Portugal; Puerto Rico: PC World Puerto Rico; Romania: Computerworld Romania, PC World Romania, Telecom Romania; Russia: Computerworld Russia, Mir PK, Sety; Singapore: Computerworld Singapore, PC World Singapore, Publish in Asia; Slovenia: MONITOR; South Africa: Computing S.A., InfoWorld S.A., Network World S.A., Software World; Spain: Computerworld Espa-a, COMUNICACIONES WORLD, Dealer World, Macworld Espa-a, PC World Espa-a; Sweden: CAP&Design, Computer Sweden, Corporate Computing, MacWorld, Maxi Data, MikroDatorn, Nätverk & Kommunikation, PC/Aktiv, PC World, Windows World; Switzerland: Computerworld Schweiz, Macworld Schweiz, PCtip; Taiwan: Computerworld Taiwan, Macworld Taiwan, PC World Taiwan, Publish Taiwan, Windows World; Thailand: Thai Computerworld, Publish in Asia; Turkey: Computerworld Turkiye, MACWORLD Turkiye, PC WORLD Turkiye; Ukraine: Computerworld Kiev, Computers & Software, Multimedia World Ukraine, PC World Ukraine; United Kingdom: Acorn User, Amiga Action, Amiga Computing, Appletalk, Computing, GamePro, Network News, Parents and Computers, PC Advisor, PC Home, PSX Pro UK, The WEB; United States: Cable in the Classroom, CD Review, CIO Magazine, Computerworld, Computerworld Client/Server Journal, Digital Video Magazine, DOS World, Federal Computer Week, GamePro, InfoWorld, I-Way, JavaWorld, Macworld, Multimedia World, Netscape World Online, Network World, PC Entertainment, PC World, Publish, SunWorld Online, SWATPro Magazine, Video Event, WebMaster; Uruguay: PC World Uruguay; Venezuela: Computerworld Venezuela, PC World Venezuela; and Vietnam: PC World Vietnam.

Every maranGraphics book represents
the extraordinary vision and commitment of a unique family:
the Maran family of Toronto, Canada.

Back Row (from left to right): *Sherry Maran, Rob Maran, Richard Maran,
Maxine Maran, Jill Maran.*

Front Row (from left to right): *Judy Maran, Ruth Maran.*

Richard Maran is the company founder and its inspirational leader. He developed maranGraphics' proprietary communication technology called "visual grammar." This book is built on that technology—empowering readers with the easiest and quickest way to learn about computers.

Ruth Maran is the Author and Architect—a role Richard established that now bears Ruth's distinctive touch. She creates the words and visual structure that are the basis for the books.

Judy Maran is the Project Coordinator. She works with Ruth, Richard and the highly talented maranGraphics illustrators, designers and editors to transform Ruth's material into its final form.

Rob Maran is the Technical and Production Specialist. He makes sure the state-of-the-art technology used to create these books always performs as it should.

Sherry Maran manages the Reception, Order Desk and any number of areas that require immediate attention and a helping hand.

Jill Maran is a jack-of-all-trades and dynamo who fills in anywhere she's needed anytime she's back from university.

Maxine Maran is the Business Manager and family sage. She maintains order in the business and family—and keeps everything running smoothly.

CREDITS

Author:
Paul Whitehead

Director of Editing & Indexer:
Kelleigh Wing

Copy Developers:
Peter Lejcar
Roxanne Van Damme
Jason M. Brown

Project Coordinator:
Judy Maran

Editors:
Tina Veltri
Raquel Scott
Janice Boyer

Layout Designer:
Jamie Bell

Illustrators:
Chris K.C. Leung
Russell C. Marini
Ben Lee
Jeff Jones
Treena J.A. Lees
Peter Grecco

Post Production:
Robert Maran

ACKNOWLEDGMENTS

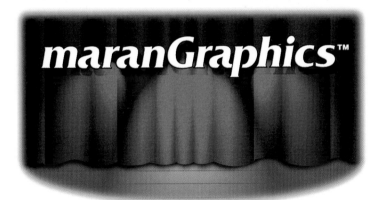

Thanks to the dedicated staff of maranGraphics, including
Jamie Bell, Janice Boyer, Jason M. Brown, Francisco Ferreira,
Peter Grecco, Brad Hilderley, Jeff Jones, Wanda Lawrie,
Ben Lee, Treena J.A. Lees, Peter Lejcar, Chris K.C. Leung,
Michael W. MᵃᶜDonald, Jill Maran, Judy Maran, Maxine Maran,
Robert Maran, Sherry Maran, Russell C. Marini, Raquel Scott,
Susanne Secko, Roxanne Van Damme, Tina Veltri,
Paul Whitehead and Kelleigh Wing.

Finally, to Richard Maran who originated the easy-to-use
graphic format of this guide. Thank you for your inspiration
and guidance.

TABLE OF CONTENTS

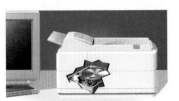

TRANSMISSION MEDIA

NETWORK ARCHITECTURE

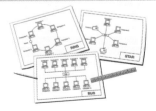

TABLE OF CONTENTS

INSTALLING OR UPGRADING A NETWORK

THE INTERNET

TABLE OF CONTENTS

CONNECTING TO THE INTERNET

INTRANETS

A network is a group of connected computers that allow people to share information and equipment, such as printers.

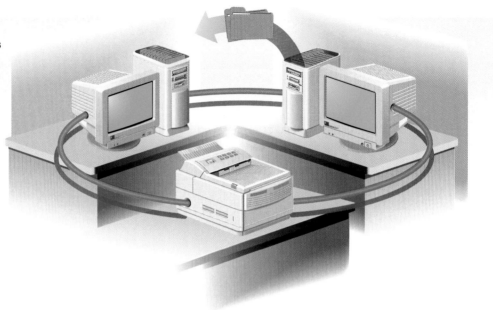

Creating a Network

A network can be any size. For example, a small business can create a network by connecting as few as two computers for sharing files.

A network can also connect millions of computers to exchange information all over the world. The world's largest network is the Internet.

Logging On

Network users are usually required to identify themselves before they can gain access to the information on a network. This is known as logging on.

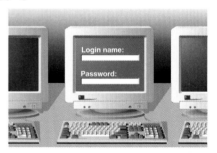

Each user must enter a personalized login name and password to access a network. By keeping this information secret, users can prevent unauthorized people from accessing the network.

NETWORK FORMATS

Sneakernet

Before networks, people used floppy disks to exchange information between computers. This method of exchanging information is known as a sneakernet. Sneakernet is slower and less reliable than a computer network. A computer network eliminates the need for sneakernet.

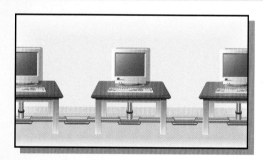

Permanent Networks

Most companies use a permanent network to transfer information. Most permanent networks use cables to link computers together. The computers and cables on a permanent network stay connected and in place at all times.

Temporary Networks

A temporary network is a network connection that is established for a brief time and then disconnected. The most common type of temporary network occurs when an employee connects a computer at home to a computer at work using a modem.

WHAT IS A NETWORK

Sharing Information

You can use a network to exchange information with other people. Information can be any form of data, such as a document created in a word processing program or information provided by a database.

Sharing Resources

Computers connected to a network can share equipment and devices, called resources. The ability to share resources reduces the cost of buying computer hardware. For example, instead of having to buy a printer for each person on a network, everyone can share one central printer.

Sharing Programs

Networks also allow people to access a copy of a program stored on a central computer, such as a spreadsheet or word processing program. Individuals can use their own computers to access and run the programs. By sharing programs, a company can avoid having to install a copy of the program on each person's computer.

Working Together

Before computer networks, many companies used one large, expensive computer to perform complex tasks. Now most companies use a network with several smaller computers. The computers on a network are less expensive and make it easier to complete complicated tasks.

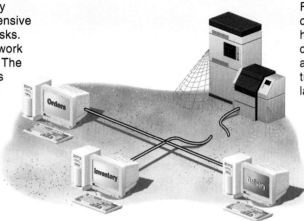

For example, multiple computers can be set up to help keep track of sales. One computer can process orders, another computer can keep track of inventory and the last can arrange for delivery.

Communication

Networks allow people to communicate and exchange messages with each other easily and efficiently. Communicating with the other people on a network is especially useful when people are working together on the same project. Messages are often delivered within seconds of being sent.

Using a network also makes it possible to hold meetings with people in another office or even on the other side of the world.

TYPES OF NETWORKS

There are many different types of networks used by businesses and organizations. Since each business and organization has its own needs, each network is unique.

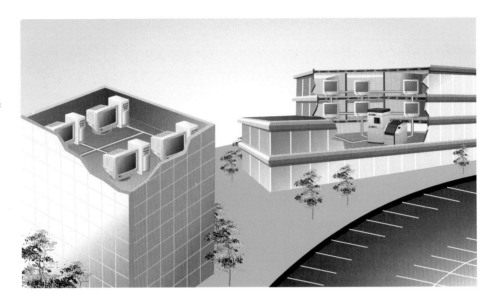

Network Size

The size of a network can often determine which type of network a business or organization should use. Different sized networks transmit data in different ways.

For example, a network with over 1,000 users is organized differently and requires a variety of components not found on a network with only five users.

Network Cost

The size and type of a network determine its cost. The larger the network, the more costly the network is to build, set up and maintain.

In addition to needing extra hardware and cables, a large network also requires specialized cabling and computers to link users and devices that are far apart.

Local Area Networks

A Local Area Network (LAN) is the most common type of network found in businesses. Local area networks connect computers and devices located close to each other, such as in one building. Usually, local area networks connect no more than 100 computers.

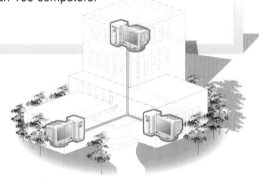

Metropolitan Area Networks

A Metropolitan Area Network (MAN) is a collection of local area networks. Metropolitan area networks connect computers located in the same geographic area, such as a city or town.

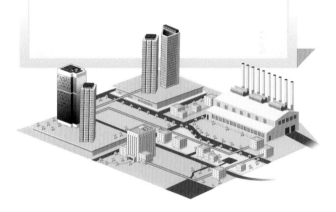

Wide Area Networks

A Wide Area Network (WAN) connects local and metropolitan area networks together. The networks that make up a wide area network may be located throughout a country or even around the world. When a single company owns and controls a wide area network, the WAN is often referred to as an enterprise network.

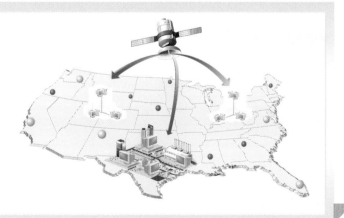

NETWORK HARDWARE

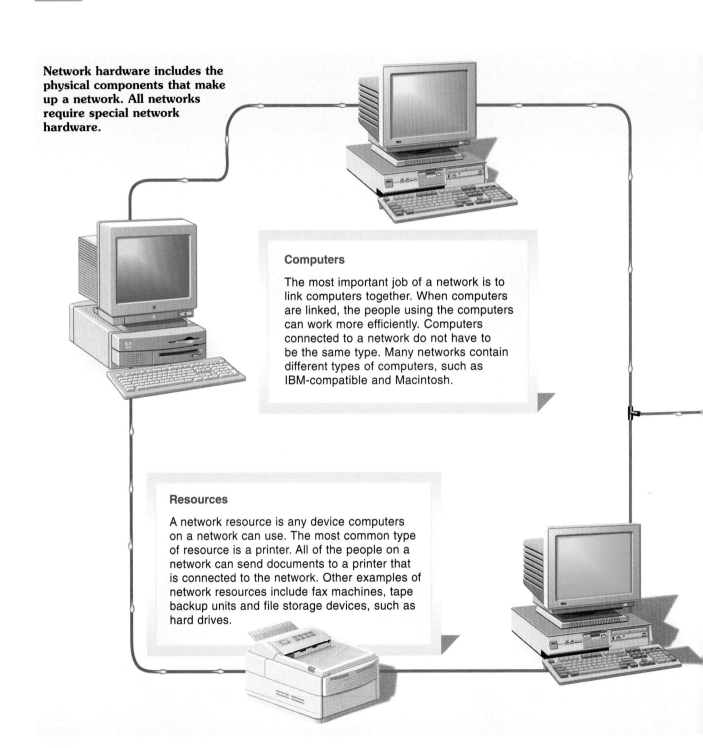

Network hardware includes the physical components that make up a network. All networks require special network hardware.

Computers

The most important job of a network is to link computers together. When computers are linked, the people using the computers can work more efficiently. Computers connected to a network do not have to be the same type. Many networks contain different types of computers, such as IBM-compatible and Macintosh.

Resources

A network resource is any device computers on a network can use. The most common type of resource is a printer. All of the people on a network can send documents to a printer that is connected to the network. Other examples of network resources include fax machines, tape backup units and file storage devices, such as hard drives.

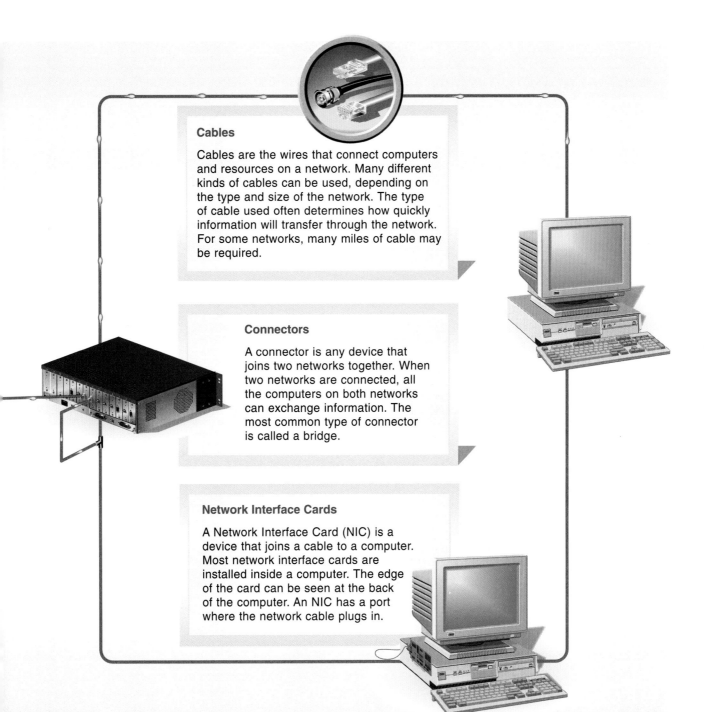

Cables

Cables are the wires that connect computers and resources on a network. Many different kinds of cables can be used, depending on the type and size of the network. The type of cable used often determines how quickly information will transfer through the network. For some networks, many miles of cable may be required.

Connectors

A connector is any device that joins two networks together. When two networks are connected, all the computers on both networks can exchange information. The most common type of connector is called a bridge.

Network Interface Cards

A Network Interface Card (NIC) is a device that joins a cable to a computer. Most network interface cards are installed inside a computer. The edge of the card can be seen at the back of the computer. An NIC has a port where the network cable plugs in.

NETWORK SOFTWARE

Network software consists of the programs run by computers connected to a network.

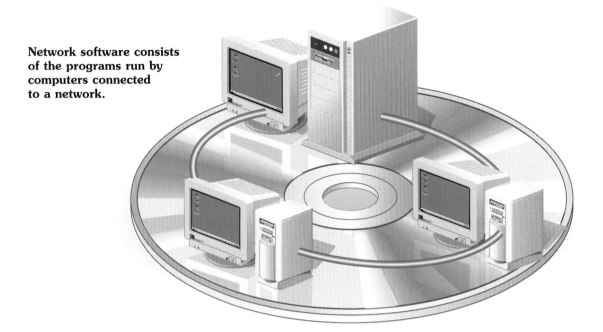

Network Operating System

The most important software on a network is the Network Operating System (NOS). The NOS organizes and manages all the activities on a network.

On most networks, one central computer is usually responsible for running the network operating system.

Network Drivers

A network driver is the software on a computer that allows the computer to use a network interface card to communicate with the network.

Application Software

Application software consists of the software that runs on computers connected to a network. Application software includes word processors, spreadsheet and drawing programs. Application software can be stored on each computer connected to the network or on a central computer that is used only for storing application software.

Server Software

A server is a computer that makes information and resources available to other computers on a network. Server software enables the server to perform a specific task. For example, mail server software allows the server to process e-mail. The server software must be compatible with the network operating system.

Management Software

Most networks that connect more than 20 computers usually run special management software. Management software allows network administrators to organize and manage a network more efficiently.

Peer-to-peer networks allow computers on a network to share their data and resources. Each computer on a peer-to-peer network stores its own information and resources. There are no central computers that control the network.

Network Size

Peer-to-peer networks work best in small environments. All the computers on the network require individual administration and maintenance, so having the network spread out over a large area can make a peer-to-peer network hard to manage.

Rule of Thumb

A peer-to-peer network should not be used if more than 10 computers will be connected together. If more than 10 computers are connected to a network, they will be easier to manage on a network that is controlled by a central computer, called a server.

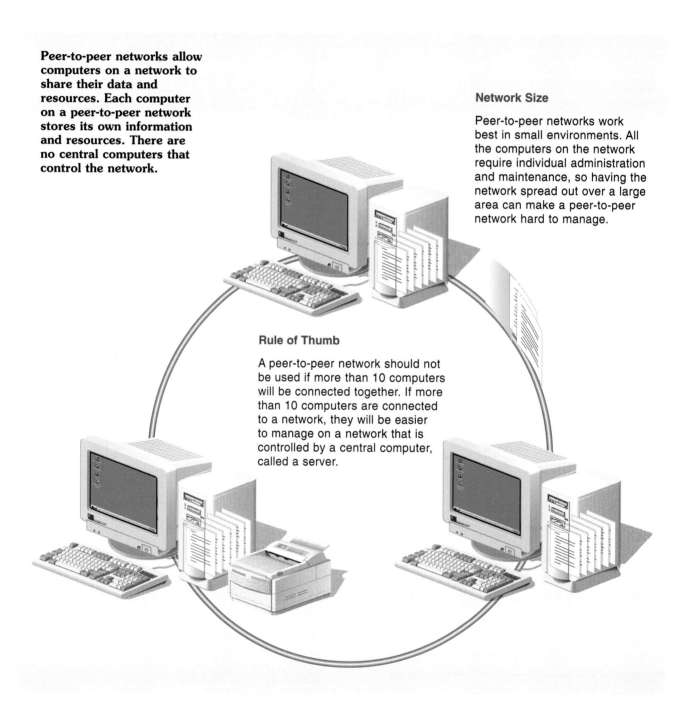

Resources

Resources such as printers and fax modems are usually connected to one computer on a peer-to-peer network. The computer then shares these resources with other computers on the network.

Programs

Most software applications, such as word processors and spreadsheet programs, used on a peer-to-peer network are installed on each computer.

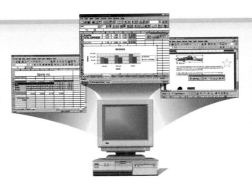

Users can use the programs on their computers to view and work with documents created by other users on the network.

Performance

When a computer is being used to provide access to information and resources, the performance of the computer can be affected. For example, if a printer is connected to a computer on a peer-to-peer network, the computer may run slower each time a user on the network prints a document.

Installation

The network operating system and all applications must be installed on each computer on a peer-to-peer network.

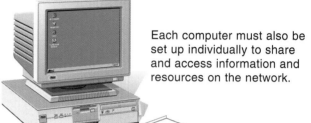

Each computer must also be set up individually to share and access information and resources on the network.

Administration

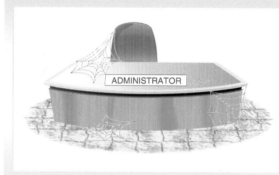

Since computers on a peer-to-peer network are configured to share and access information individually, users will have to learn how to administer their own computers. There is usually no dedicated system administrator for a peer-to-peer network.

Security

Since users on a peer-to-peer network store files and information on their own computers, anyone may be able to access the information on another user's computer by using that computer. This makes information on a peer-to-peer network less secure than a network where information is stored in a central location.

Cost

The cost of a peer-to-peer network is generally lower than other types of networks when only a few computers are being connected.

As a peer-to-peer network grows, the system becomes more expensive than other types of networks.

Advanced Features

Peer-to-peer networks are often used to let people share information and resources such as printers and fax modems.

Peer-to-peer networks often do not offer features found in more advanced networks, such as office e-mail and remote access.

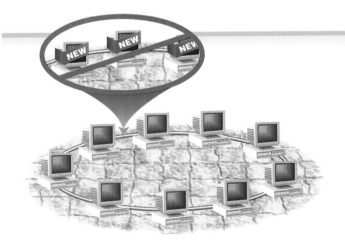

Expansion

Peer-to-peer networks should only be used in situations where the network is not expected to grow in size. Many peer-to-peer networks have to be replaced when they grow to include several more computers.

CLIENT/SERVER NETWORKS

Client/server networks are created using a central computer that serves information to other computers, which are referred to as clients. A client/server network is often the most efficient way to connect 10 or more computers.

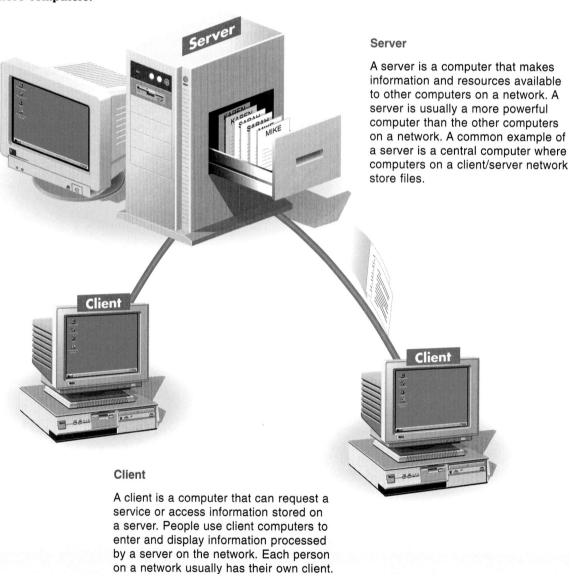

Server

A server is a computer that makes information and resources available to other computers on a network. A server is usually a more powerful computer than the other computers on a network. A common example of a server is a central computer where computers on a client/server network store files.

Client

A client is a computer that can request a service or access information stored on a server. People use client computers to enter and display information processed by a server on the network. Each person on a network usually has their own client.

Efficiency

On a client/server network, servers perform most of the processing and resource-intensive tasks. Servers are powerful computers that are better suited to performing complex tasks than client computers.

Services

A server is usually dedicated to providing one specific service to clients on the network. For example, a file server stores and manages all the files on a network. A print server controls printing for all the clients on a network. A database server stores and organizes large amounts of information.

Programs

One of the most popular uses of a client/server network is to store programs on a server that other computers on the network may use. For example, a server may store a copy of a drawing program. When users want to run the drawing program, they can run the program from the server.

CLIENT/SERVER NETWORKS

Size

Client/server networks can be used with any size of network, but are especially suited for large networks. This type of network is easy to set up and can be configured to meet most of the requirements of large companies.

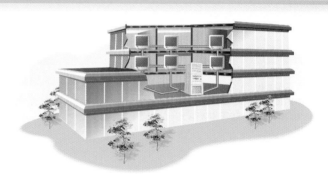

Administration

Networks need some tasks to be performed on a daily basis, such as data backups and security monitoring. Most client/server networks have a network administrator to take care of the daily administrative tasks.

Client/server networks are relatively easy to maintain and manage because the servers are usually located in one central area.

Security

Most servers on a client/server network are always turned on and must be protected from interference, such as someone changing the settings of the server. Most companies store network servers in a separate room that can be locked.

Expansion

A server uses most of the complicated software and hardware in a network. It is easy to add client computers to a network because clients do not need complex hardware and software.

Repair

It is usually easy to find the source of a problem on a client/server network. If many client computers are having problems, the cause is often the server.

If only one client computer is having a problem, the client can easily be replaced with another computer.

Cost

Client/server networks save money by using computers for the tasks for which they are best suited. The more powerful computers are used as servers. Less expensive and less powerful computers are used as client computers.

NETWORK BENEFITS

Many companies have discovered that there are several benefits to connecting computers together. Networks can improve the way companies operate by increasing productivity, lowering costs and much more.

Productivity

Ease of Access

Many networks store most information on a central computer. Storing information on a central computer makes it easy for people to work with and manage their files.

A network also allows people to access their information from other computers on the network.

Work from Home

Many networks have dedicated computers that allow people to connect to the company's network using a modem and another computer outside the network.

Once users are connected to the network, they can work with any data stored on the network. Networks make it easy for people to access office information from home.

Productivity

Using computers connected to a network lets people exchange information with each other. When employees can easily access and exchange information, they can work more efficiently. For example, networks allow people in different offices to work on a project together.

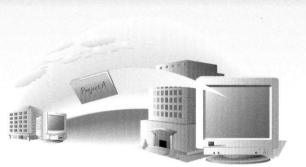

Programs

Most people who are connected to a network use a central computer to work with programs such as word processors and spreadsheet programs. Networks make installing programs simple because only one copy of a program needs to be installed on a central computer.

Cost

Before networks, a printer was usually attached to each computer in an office. Networks allow computers to share many types of resources, including printers and hard drives. The ability to share equipment reduces the cost of buying computer hardware.

Administration

Networks make it easy to monitor and control who uses a company's computers. Many companies have one person, the network administrator, who oversees all administration for the network.

Before users can access information on a network, they must enter a user name and a password. This ensures that only authorized people can use the information stored on the network. User names and passwords allow the network administrator to keep track of everyone who uses the computers on a network.

NETWORK ADMINISTRATOR

Security

Most networks have built-in security programs. These security programs can monitor and report any abnormal activity on a network computer to the network administrator.

ACCESS DENIED

Many networks can be set up to refuse access to anyone who enters an incorrect password. This discourages unauthorized users from trying to access information on the network.

Reliability

Most networks are designed to be durable and can operate uninterrupted for long periods of time. Once a network is running, very little work is needed to keep the network operating.

Some networks can even alert the network administrator if a problem develops on the network.

Backup

Many companies use networks to back up employees' information. Employees can save their information on a central computer used only for storing data.

When a backup is performed, only the information on the server needs to be backed up. Backing up information from a central location on a network is more reliable and secure than backing up data on each user's computer.

Protection of Information

Usually only a few computers are used to store most of the files and information on a network. These computers can be kept in a secure location, such as a locked room.

Protecting these computers and the information they store makes it easier for a company to recover from disasters such as fire or theft.

NETWORK CONSIDERATIONS

Before a company installs a new network or upgrades its existing network, there are many factors to consider.

Planning

When planning to install a new network or upgrade an existing network, it is important to evaluate each type of network by reading network publications and by talking to other people who have installed and used networks.

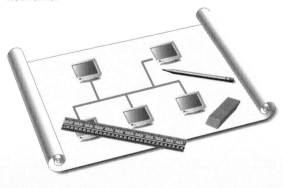

Suitability to Task

Different types of networks are better suited for different types of tasks. Before installing or upgrading a network, a company should determine what types of tasks the network will perform.

For example, a rapidly expanding company that needs to exchange files with a branch office across the country will require a different type of network than a small company that exchanges files between a few computers.

Ease of Use

Networks can be very complicated and require the user to enter large amounts of information before accessing the network. The network operating system should make the network easy to use. At most, a user should only need to enter a login name and password to access the network.

Administration

Most networks require administration and maintenance on a regular basis. If the network is hard to use and maintain, a highly-skilled person will be required to administer the network. If the network is easy to use, maintenance may be done by any user or employee.

Security

Once a computer is connected to a network, the computer can be accessed by any device or computer connected to the network.

A good network will have built-in security features that make it difficult to access a computer or device without proper authorization.

Cost

An important consideration when installing or upgrading a network is the cost. A network should save a company money by making better use of existing resources, such as printers and hard drives. A network should also increase employee productivity by providing better access to company data.

Installation

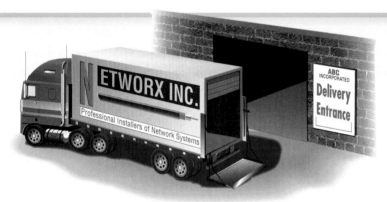

Many networks can be very complex to install and configure. A large network may take weeks to install, while a small network may take only a few hours. Networks should always be installed by qualified technicians.

Service

Mechanical and system errors can often occur on networks. Once installed, a network should be well-maintained. Most companies and organizations have employees dedicated to servicing the network. Some businesses hire people from third party companies to service their networks.

Flexibility

A network must be able to grow and change along with the business or organization that uses it. Some networks have limits on the number of computers that can be attached to the network. A limited network should not be used in a company that plans to expand in the future.

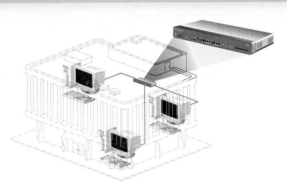

Compatibility

Networks often grow to the point where they will be attached to another network, like the Internet, or to other networks within the same company.

A well-planned network will be able to easily connect to and exchange information with other types of networks.

Add-on Features

Many networks allow people to purchase and add on different networking features. Some companies may need to consider add-on features if they anticipate future growth. Some common add-on features of a network include network administration packages, fax machine servers and CD-ROM servers.

CHAPTER 2

Network Structure

Before setting up a network, it is important to consider the network layout. This chapter discusses four main types of network structures used today.

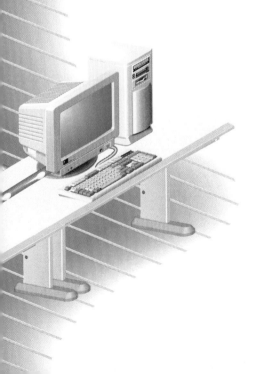

INTRODUCTION TO NETWORK STRUCTURE

Network structure, also called network topology, indicates how a network is designed or laid out. A network structure has both a physical level and a logical level.

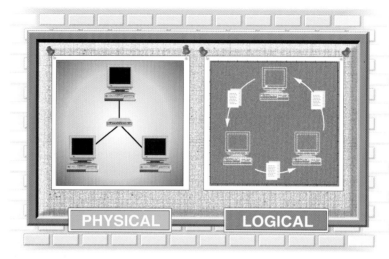

PHYSICAL   LOGICAL

The four main types of network structures are bus, star, ring and hybrid. For information on each network structure, see pages 32 to 39.

PHYSICAL LEVEL

The physical level identifies the parts of a network that physically exist, such as the computers, cables and connectors. This level also specifies where the computers on a network are located and how all the parts of the network are connected.

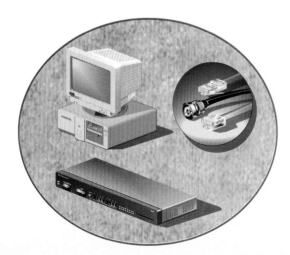

The Physical Transfer of Information

A network must have some form of transmission media to transfer information. Many networks exchange information by using cables.

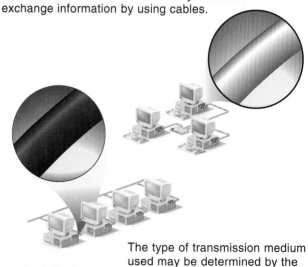

The type of transmission medium used may be determined by the network's physical structure.

LOGICAL LEVEL

The logical level identifies how information moves through a network. The logical level is determined by many factors. One logical structure might work well for transferring large files, while another might be more suitable for networks that transfer mostly small files.

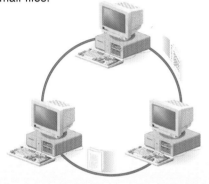

The Logical Transfer of Information

Computers communicate by exchanging electric signals. Signals are transferred through the transmission media that connects the computers. Signals may take different routes, depending on how the network is connected.

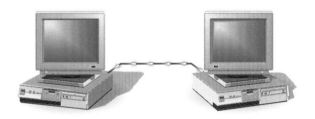

COMBINED NETWORK STRUCTURES

Networks frequently use the same type of network structure for both the logical and physical levels. However, some networks use a different structure for each level. For example, a network may use a logical ring network with a physical star network.

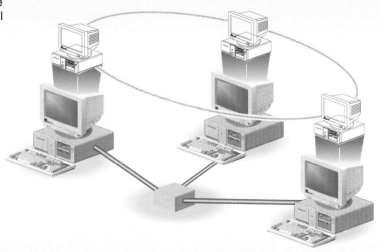

BUS NETWORK STRUCTURE

A bus network consists of a continuous length of cable that connects two or more devices together. A bus network is also called a backbone network.

How Information Transfers

On a bus network, only one computer can transfer information at a time. When a computer sends information, the information moves through the entire length of the cable. The destination computer must retrieve the information from the cable.

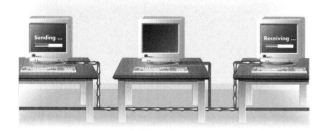

Terminators

A terminator is a device that absorbs the signals transmitted on a network cable. Each end of the cable on a bus network must have a terminator. Terminators prevent signals from being bounced back along the cable and causing interference.

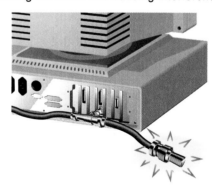

The type of terminator required depends on the type of cable used on the network.

Setup

The setup of a bus network is simple. Each computer must be connected to a single length of cable. A bus network is often used to connect a few computers located in a small area, such as an office.

Expansion

Expanding an existing bus network can be difficult. When adding a computer to a bus network, the cable must be broken to extend the cable and attach the computer.

The other computers on the network cannot exchange information while the cable is broken.

Repair

If a computer is malfunctioning and causing a problem on the cable, the entire network will be affected. This can make the cause of a problem difficult to isolate and repair.

Cost

Bus networks are quite inexpensive. Most bus networks use a single piece of copper cable to connect its computers together.

STAR NETWORK STRUCTURE

A star network structure consists
of individual computers connected
to a central point on the network.
Star networks are the most
common type of network.

How Information Transfers

In a star network, each computer
is connected to a central network
connector, called a hub. All
information that transfers from
one computer to another on the
network passes through the hub.

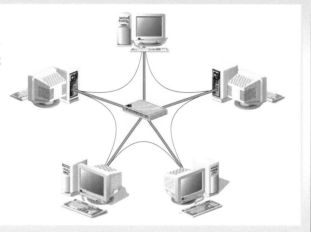

Setup

Each computer in a star network must
be relatively close to the network
hub. Cable lengths between a
computer and the hub should
be less than 100 meters.
Hubs commonly connect 4,
8 or 16 computers together.
In a large office building, it is
common for each floor of the
building to have its own hub.

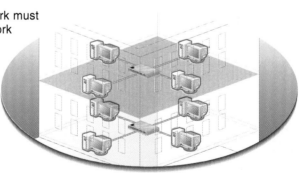

Expansion

As long as there is a free port on the hub, only a cable is needed to connect another computer to a star network. The network does not need to be shut down when new computers are connected.

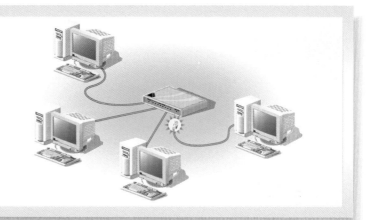

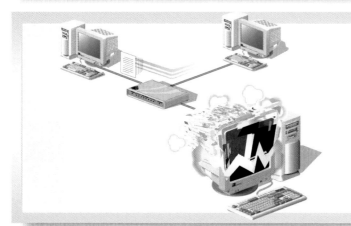

Troubleshooting

When an error occurs on a computer or cable, the rest of the network is unaffected. Many hubs are capable of detecting network problems and isolating these areas from the rest of the network. When a hub fails, information can no longer transfer from one computer to another.

Cost

Star networks cost more to implement than other types of networks. Each computer must be connected to a network hub, an expensive component of a star network. Large amounts of cable are also used in star networks because each computer on the network must be independently connected to the hub.

RING NETWORK STRUCTURE

A ring network structure consists of individual computers connected to a single length of cable arranged in a ring.

How Information Transfers

The information on a ring network travels in one direction only. When a computer transfers information, it sends the information to the computer located next to it.

If a computer receives information that is not addressed to it, the computer passes the information to the next computer along the ring. The computers continue to pass the information until it reaches the intended destination.

Setup

A ring network is often used to connect computers that are located close to each other. All the computers on a ring network must be attached to a single ring of cable. There is no beginning or end in a ring network.

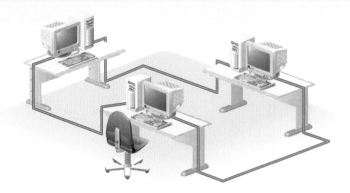

Expansion

Expanding a ring network may be more difficult than expanding other types of networks. When adding a new computer to a ring network, the cable must be broken to attach the computer. The network will not be functional until the new computer is connected.

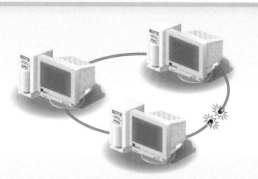

Troubleshooting

When a break in the ring occurs, all computers before the break will be able to exchange information, while those after the break will not. This makes it easy to determine the location of the faulty connection.

Many ring networks have dual rings that transmit information in different directions to help prevent network shutdowns.

Cost

Ring networks can be slightly more expensive to set up than other types of networks. Since all the computers on a ring network must be attached to a single ring of cable, the network will require a greater amount of cable if the computers are far apart.

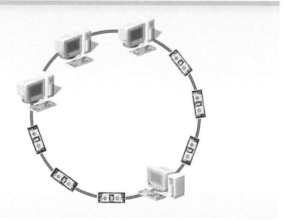

HYBRID NETWORK STRUCTURE

A hybrid network structure uses a mixture of many different kinds of network structures.

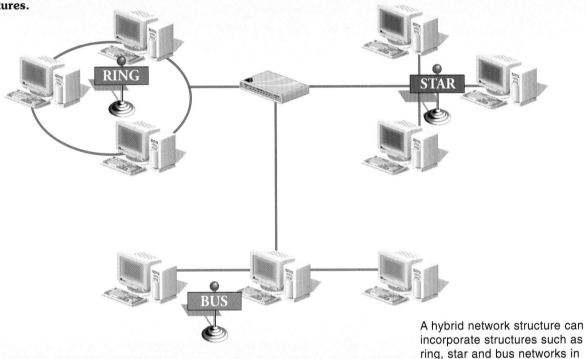

A hybrid network structure can incorporate structures such as ring, star and bus networks in one large network.

Wide Area Networks

Wide Area Networks (WANs) are the most common examples of hybrid networks. WANs incorporate many different kinds of network structures by connecting multiple networks together. The networks that make up a wide area network may be located throughout a country or even around the world.

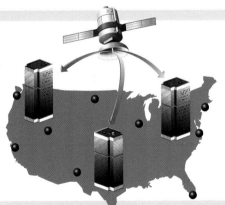

For example, a company may use a star or bus network to connect computers within individual offices. These office networks may then be connected by a microwave or satellite-based network to offices on the other side of the country.

Remote Access

One of the most common features of a hybrid network is the ability to let users access information on the network while at home or traveling.

People can use computers with modems to connect to the network and then access information and resources as if they were directly connected to the network.

Management

A hybrid network uses many different technologies and therefore can be difficult to manage and administrate.

A company that uses a large hybrid network usually has its own network support department that is responsible for managing and maintaining the network.

Cost

Hybrid networks are usually expensive because they are large, complicated networks. Some hybrid networks may need more safety features than other networks because they span large distances.

A backup network structure may also be required with a hybrid network, which can increase cost. For example, a company may connect its offices by satellite, but also have a cable connection in case of a failure.

NETWORK LAYOUTS

CENTRALIZED NETWORK LAYOUT

A centralized network layout places most of its important resources, such as file servers, in one central location.

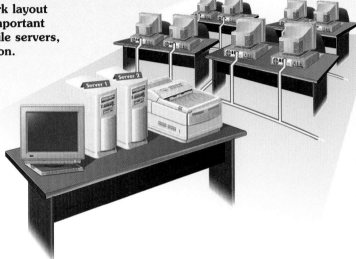

The bus, ring, star and hybrid structures can all be used with a centralized network layout.

Administration

Administration is easier on a centralized network than on a network that does not centralize its resources. On many centralized networks, most of the important resources, such as file and database servers, are placed in one location that may be locked.

Placing the resources in a locked location can help keep the resources safe from theft and fire.

Backup

All files on a network should be regularly backed up. Regular backups prevent the loss of information if something happens to the computers that the files are stored on.

It is usually easier to back up files that are stored in one central location than it is to back up files on each user's computer.

Speed

Most of the equipment in a
centralized network is built
specifically for powerful
processing work. The
equipment is often built to
operate faster than ordinary
computer equipment.

For example, hard drives used
in file servers are often faster
than hard drives used in
desktop computers.

Reliability

Most networks are very reliable.
However, the problem with having
resources placed in one location
is that if a server fails, many
people will be affected.

Some network administrators
create a duplicate server, called
a mirror server, to act as a
backup to the main server.

Cost

Although centralized networks can
seem very expensive to construct,
they can be an inexpensive way
to provide computer services to
a large number of people.

NETWORK LAYOUTS

A distributed network layout places the most important functions, such as file and printer sharing, throughout the network. For example, each department in a company may have its own file and print servers.

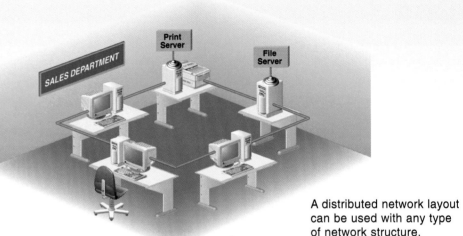

A distributed network layout can be used with any type of network structure.

Powerful

A distributed network can use the processing power of many computers to complete a task. For example, a network designed to process information in a database may consist of many computers, each performing a specific task. One computer could perform calculations, the other process information and the last print the information.

A single computer performing the entire task may be overwhelmed by the large volume of work.

Administration

Administration on a distributed network can be quite difficult. Each user on the network can request resources from the network.

People who use a distributed network often have to know more about the operating system used on the network than people on a centralized network.

Backup

Backing up information on a distributed network can be complex. The files must be backed up on each computer connected to the network. Computers connected to a distributed network often have their own backup devices. Portable tape backup devices that can be shared by several users are popular.

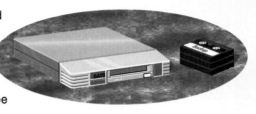

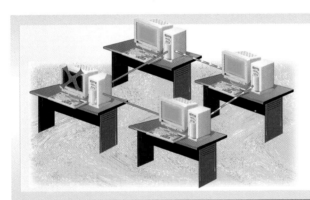

Reliable

Distributed networks are relatively safe in the event of a computer failure. When one computer fails, it usually affects only a small number of users on the network.

Cost

A distributed network layout may cost less than a centralized network layout because there is no need for expensive servers. Desktop computers used on a distributed network may need to be more powerful than regular desktop computers.

100
Mbps

CHAPTER 3

Network Hardware

This chapter explains the physical
devices needed to construct and
operate a network. Learn about the
importance of servers, how bridges
may ease an overloaded network,
how routers direct information and
much more.

SERVERS

Servers are powerful computers that perform specific tasks on a network.

Planning

Most servers are designed to be upgraded and improved throughout their lifespan. Before installing a server, it is important to determine the future needs of the server. Many servers have limits on the amount of memory and processor types that can be installed. The network administrator should plan ahead so that servers do not have to be replaced with newer models when inexpensive upgrades could be performed.

Speed

The speed of a server is determined by many factors. The two major factors that determine the speed of a server are the amount of memory in the server and the type of Central Processing Unit (CPU). Servers often use the latest and fastest central processing units.

Memory

Most desktop computers can operate with 16 megabytes (MB) of memory. Servers often have at least 64 megabytes (MB) of memory and could have gigabytes (GB) of memory installed.

In most cases, the more memory a server has, the more efficiently the server will run.

Storage

The storage system is one of the main components of a computer system. Most servers have access to large storage devices because servers tend to run large programs and store a lot of information.

Operating System

The operating system on a server is often determined by the applications or tasks that the server runs. Some applications may only be available for one type of operating system.

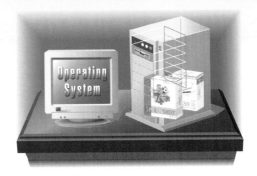

The applications on the server must be compatible with the operating system that runs on the server.

Fault Tolerance

A network server is often used by many people. If a problem occurs with the server, it could affect the work of all the users. There are several ways to ensure that the server will not fail or lose power.

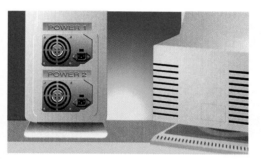

For example, a server may have two power supplies, so if one breaks down, the other will still be available to supply power to the server.

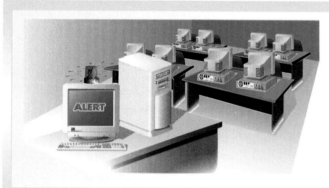

Notification

Many servers have a notification system that can alert the network administrator if a problem develops. Some servers have a modem connected to a telephone line that allows the server to automatically send a message to the pager of the network administrator when there is a problem.

Security

Servers often have security devices to protect them from interference by unauthorized users. The keyboards on most servers can be disabled while running. To reactivate the server, a password must be entered.

Most companies also store their servers in a separate room that can be locked.

Maintenance

Servers should be shut down regularly for maintenance. Maintenance often involves nothing more than running a program that checks to make sure the server is still functioning optimally.

Repair

Just like all computers, there will be a time when a server will need repair. Servers are often designed to make repair simple, with features like easy-access panels to allow fast access to critical areas, such as hard drives.

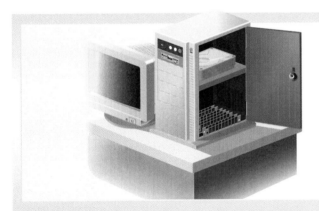

Online Repair

Many servers in large companies must run all the time. This can cause a problem if the server needs a component, such as the memory, to be replaced or upgraded.

Some advanced servers allow components such as adapter cards, power supplies and memory to be removed and replaced while the server is still running.

NETWORK COMPUTERS

Network computers are basic computers designed to be used on a network. Network computers are also referred to as thin-clients or NCs.

Hardware and Software

Network computers are the same as regular computers but cost less because they have much less hardware and software installed. Most network computers include a monitor and a built-in network interface card to allow the computer to connect to the network. Due to the lack of hardware and software, network computers require less administrative support than regular personal computers.

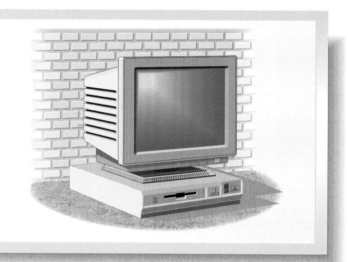

Client/Server Networks

Network computers are found on client/server networks. A central application server provides most of the applications that the network computer can run, such as a word processor or spreadsheet program.

JAVA

Java is a programming language that is used extensively on network computers.

Java Applications

Applications such as a word processor or database program can be written in Java and stored on a server on a network. Java applications can run on most types of computers, no matter which operating system the computer uses. Using Java applications can reduce the cost of a network because all users can work with the same program. The company does not need to purchase a copy of the program for each type of operating system.

Network Computer Requirements

When Java applications are used on a network, the network computers only need to be able to work with Java. The network computers do not need a large amount of storage space and memory. Most network computers only need enough power and equipment to connect to the network, access the server and run Java.

STORAGE DEVICES

Most networks use a file server to store files and information on the network. All file servers must have a storage device.

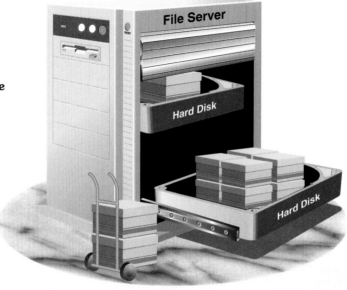

The type of storage device used depends on the type and size of data being stored.

Connecting

Most storage devices are connected directly to the file server. The storage device and the file server must connect using the same method. Small Computer Systems Interface (SCSI, pronounced "scuzzy") is the most common way to connect storage devices to a file server.

Hard Disk Drives

Hard disk drives are the central storage devices on most file servers. Hard disk drives are fast, but they are expensive compared to other storage devices. Because they are used more frequently, the hard disk drives on a file server must be larger and more reliable than the hard disk drives on a desktop computer.

Compact Discs

Compact discs can store large amounts of information, but once recorded, the information cannot be modified. Compact discs on a file server are most often used for retrieving information.

Many companies use compact discs to allow users to access a large quantity of reference materials, such as medical or legal information.

Tapes

Tapes have been used for decades as a reliable way to create backup copies of computer information. The network's system administrator can use a backup program to automatically back up information onto tapes when the file server is not busy, such as at night. A tape drive can store more information than any other storage medium.

Optical Drives

Some optical drives can record information. Recordable optical drives are often used for storing rarely used information. Compared to other types of storage devices, optical drives tend to be slow, but have a high storage capacity.

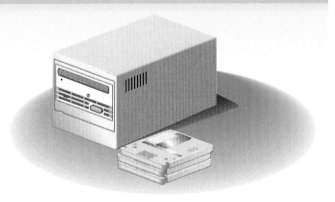

NETWORK PRINTERS

The ability to share printers was one of the original reasons computers were joined together by networks.

Sharing

Many people can share a network printer. If everyone on a network uses the same network printer, the printer may take a long time to produce print jobs. Access to a printer can be restricted to a specific group of people if the network is too large to share one printer.

Print Servers

Print servers are computers used to manage and store print jobs that are going to be printed by a network printer. A print server often manages print jobs for several network printers. On many networks, the print server is directly connected to the printer.

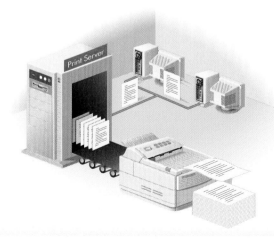

Installation

Most network printers can be attached directly to the network using a network adapter. The network cable plugs into the network adapter at the back of the printer.

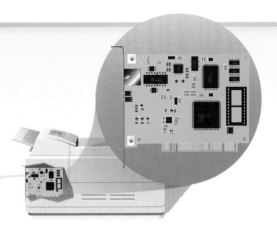

Most network printers can be attached to several different types of networks.

Cost

Network printers can be very expensive. Although it can cost many times more than a standard printer, a network printer is a better alternative to a standard printer.

Without a network printer, each user on the network would require their own printer.

Maintenance

Network printers have demanding maintenance schedules. The internal mechanisms of a network printer need to be maintained on a regular basis, usually after a certain number of pages have been printed.

Many network printers will no longer print documents if regular maintenance is not performed.

Paper Capacity

Before purchasing a network printer, make sure it has a large enough paper capacity to meet the demands of the network. Most network printers have a paper capacity of at least 500 pages.

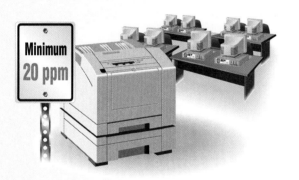

Printer Speed

Network printers have to be very fast if several people use them to print large quantities of documents. A good network laser printer will print at a speed of at least 20 pages per minute. A slow network printer will lead to backlogs and decreased productivity.

Print Quality

Most network printers are capable of printing high-quality documents. Many network laser printers can print at resolutions of over 600 dots per inch (dpi). A resolution of 600 dpi is suitable for most types of office documents.

Features

Network printers have become increasingly sophisticated over the past few years. Many network printers sort print jobs into different piles to make it easier for people to retrieve their print jobs.

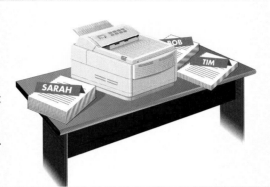

Some larger network printers are even capable of sorting and stapling print jobs.

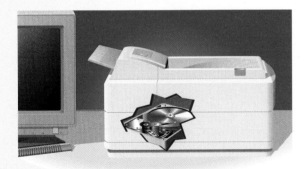

Built-in Hard Drives

Many network printers have built-in hard drives that store print jobs in a print queue until the printer is ready to process them. It may be possible for a system administrator to remove print jobs from the hard drive or schedule a print job to print at a specific time.

Reliability

Network printers are more reliable than standard printers because they are designed to work for extended periods of time without breaking down.

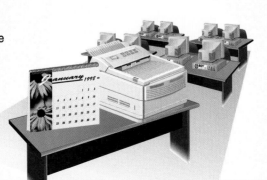

Since many users share network printers, a breakdown in a network printer could affect many people.

NETWORK INTERFACE CARDS

A Network Interface Card (NIC) physically connects a computer to the transmission medium used on a network. A network interface card controls the flow of information between a computer and the network.

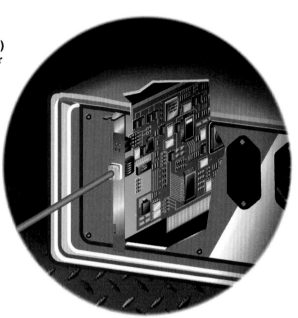

Servers

Servers are usually the busiest computers on a network. The network interface cards used by servers are often high performance devices that have been specifically designed to transfer large amounts of data.

Addressing

Every network interface card has its own unique hardware address. The hardware address is set when the network interface card is manufactured. The hardware address is used to identify each network interface card when information is being sent or received on the network.

Cables

Network interface cards that connect to cables are designed to use a specific type of network cable. The type of cable used on the network and the amount of information the cable can transfer at once are factors that determine the type of network interface card required.

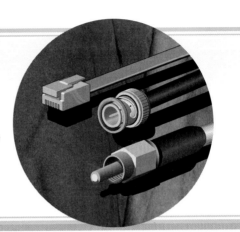

Transceivers

A transceiver is the part of a network interface card that translates information from the signals that the computer understands to signals that can transfer on the network.

Older transceivers attached directly to the network cable and then connected to the network interface card. Most network interface cards now have built-in transceivers.

Boot Chips

Some computers connected to a network may not have their own disk drives. In order to access the network, a special computer chip called a boot chip, or boot PROM, is attached to the network interface card. The boot chip lets the network interface card connect to the network.

NETWORK INTERFACE CARDS

Installing a Network Interface Card

Most network interface cards are installed directly into a computer. A computer has internal connectors called expansion slots that allow the network interface card to be inserted into the computer.

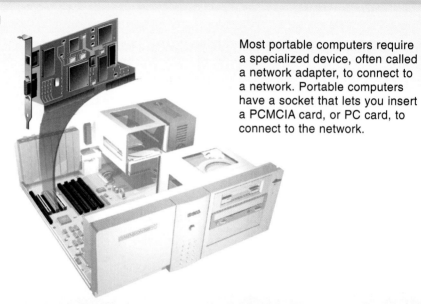

Most portable computers require a specialized device, often called a network adapter, to connect to a network. Portable computers have a socket that lets you insert a PCMCIA card, or PC card, to connect to the network.

Ports

A port is used to connect the network interface card to the network. Each network interface card has at least one port, and in some cases two ports, that enable it to connect to a network using one or two different cable types.

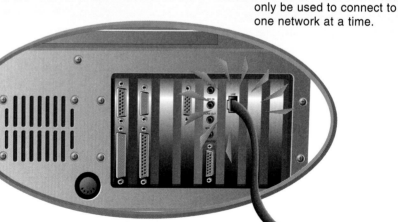

A network interface card can only be used to connect to one network at a time.

Device Drivers

Before a network interface card can be used by an operating system, it needs special software called device drivers installed on the computer. Device drivers allow the network interface card to communicate with the operating system.

Each network interface card and operating system requires a specific device driver. Device drivers cannot be interchanged.

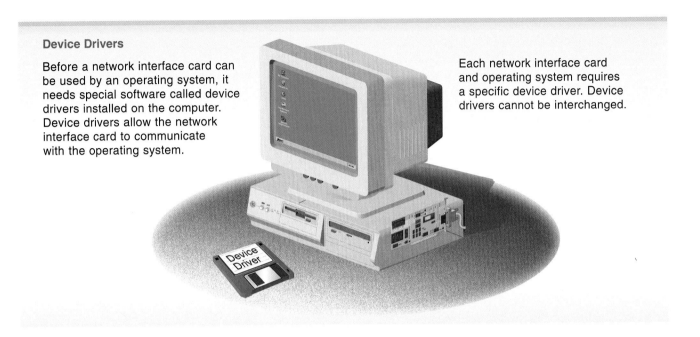

Configuring a Network Interface Card

There are many settings that may have to be adjusted before using a network interface card in a computer. The Memory Range lets the network interface card communicate directly with the computer's memory to speed the processing of information.

The Interrupt Request (IRQ) is used to tell the computer when the network interface card needs attention. The Input/Output (I/O) Range indicates which areas of memory the network interface card uses to communicate with the computer. Some operating systems will automatically configure the network interface card.

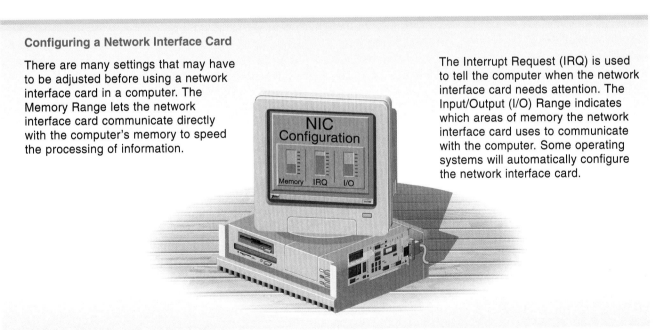

HUBS

A hub provides a central location where all the cables on a network come together. Hubs are found on most modern networks.

Passive Hubs

A passive hub connects wires on a network in one central location. Passive hubs do not process information because they do not contain any circuitry or electrical devices. The main function of a passive hub is to connect the wires in the network.

Active Hubs

An active hub can regenerate a signal as the signal passes through the hub. Signal regeneration helps to eliminate errors on the network that are caused by electrical interference. Active hubs are more expensive than passive hubs.

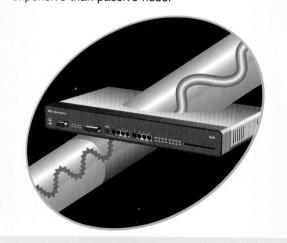

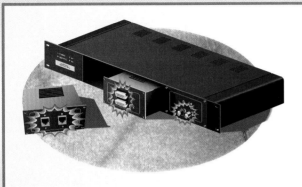

Transmission Medium

Most network hubs are designed to operate with one type of transmission medium, such as fiber-optic cable. However, some hubs can be modified to accept connections from different types of transmission media. These hubs are sometimes referred to as modular hubs.

Connections

Computer devices are most often connected to a hub using cables. In many offices, the cables are pre-wired into the walls from the hub to a socket on the wall.

When a computer needs to be connected to the network, the computer can simply be plugged into a socket.

Ports

Computer devices connect to the hub through a connector, called a port. Common hubs have 4, 8 or 16 ports. Usually each port has an indicator light, called a Light Emitting Diode (LED), which lights up when a computer is attached to the port and turned on. Some LEDs indicate when information is being transferred through the port.

Fault Tolerance

Hubs are an important part of a network, so it is important that they can operate continuously. Many hubs have built-in features, such as dual power supplies, that prevent the hub from shutting down when a component in the hub fails.

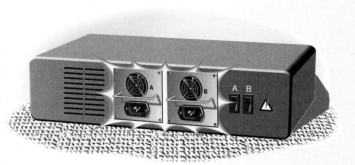

Switching Hubs

If a network is slowed down by many users, a switching hub can restore the network to its original performance. Switching hubs are slowly replacing routers and bridges used on networks.

Management

Many hubs now have built-in management functions which allow the hub to be administered and configured from a central computer. The ports on a hub can be disabled or enabled using management functions.

Management functions may also help a network administrator monitor hubs to determine potential sources of trouble.

Network Structures

Traditionally, only star network structures used hubs. Using hubs to connect computers is now very common. Many types of network structures, such as ring networks, are now using hubs as the primary method of connecting computers.

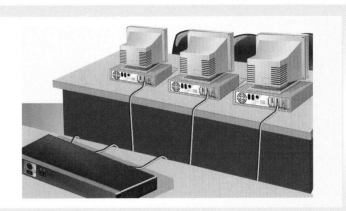

Daisy Chaining

Most hubs can attach up to 16 computers. A network that has more than 16 computers can use two or more hubs connected together. Connecting two or more hubs is referred to as daisy chaining.

Reconfiguration

If a network uses a series of hubs, it is simple to add, move or remove a computer on the network. A cable can easily be removed from a socket, or port, on one hub and plugged into a port on another hub. The network does not need to be shut down or disrupted during reconfiguration.

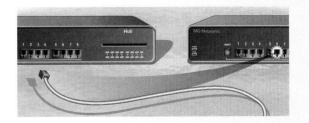

REPEATERS

A repeater is a connector that takes a signal that is being transferred on a network and re-transmits the information. Repeaters allow signals to travel farther along a network.

Network Extension

Repeaters are used to extend the length of transmission media, such as cables, which connects computer devices together on a network. Repeaters are especially useful in areas where long lengths of cables are required to connect the computer devices together, such as a network in a large warehouse.

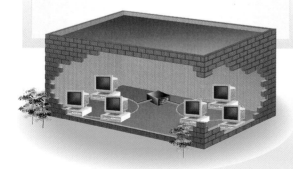

Network Restrictions

Repeaters are very simple devices that do not operate efficiently when they have to transfer large amounts of information. Repeaters should not be used to extend the length of a busy network.

Degraded Signals

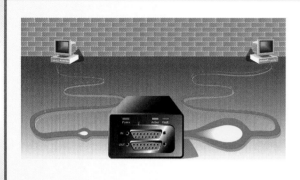

The further a signal has to travel along a cable, the weaker the signal will become. Signal degradation is often referred to as attenuation. By re-transmitting the signal, repeaters fix any problems with a network that are caused by weak signals.

Signal Amplification

A repeater is used to strengthen the signal it receives. The repeater then re-transmits the amplified signal along the network cable. Amplified signals can travel along a longer length of cable.

Signal Regeneration

To avoid transmitting interference and other errors on the network cable, most repeaters filter out any interference or distortion before they amplify and re-transmit the signal. This process is referred to as signal regeneration.

A bridge is a device that allows the computers on individual networks or separate parts of a network to exchange information.

Create Internetworks

Bridges are used to connect a small number of individual networks to make them work together as one large network.

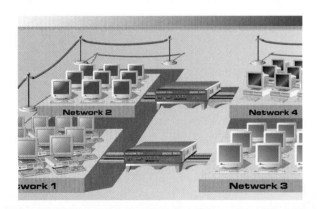

A network made up of smaller networks is called an internetwork.

Divide Networks

Bridges are also used to split an overloaded network into smaller parts. Splitting an overloaded network reduces the amount of information transferring in each part of the network.

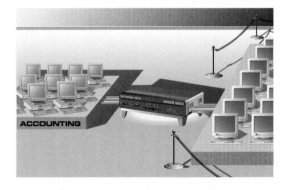

For example, if a lot of information is being transferred between computers in one department, a bridge can separate that department from the rest of the network. Both parts of the network will then operate more efficiently.

Filtering

Bridges determine if information is going to a destination on the same network or to the network on the other side of the bridge. If the destination is on the network on the other side of the bridge, the bridge forwards the information to that network.

A bridge improves efficiency because information is only forwarded to a different network when necessary.

Learning Bridges

Each computer on a network has a unique address that is used to identify the computer when it sends or receives information.

In order to efficiently filter and transfer information, a bridge must know the address of each computer on the network. Learning bridges can read and store, or learn, the address of each computer that sends information on the network.

Connect Similar Networks

Bridges can only transfer information from one network to another.

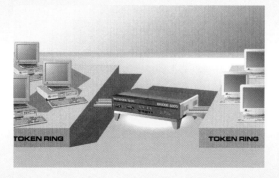

Since bridges cannot change the information in any way, bridges can only connect similar types of networks.

Routers are connectors that are used to link different networks together. Routers can direct, or route, information to the correct destination.

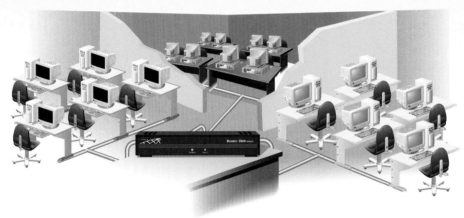

On a large network, there may be more than one route that information can take to get to its destination.

Redundant Paths

Routes that are not normally used to transfer information are called redundant paths. If a section of the network has been shut down for maintenance or due to malfunction, then the redundant paths can be used to transfer information.

Intelligent Routers

Some routers can automatically detect if a part of the network is not working or is slow. The routers will try to redirect information around the problem area so the impact of the network failure will be minimal. Routers that can determine the best route for information to take are often called intelligent routers.

Setting Up Routers

Information such as the name of the router and what types of networks are attached to the router must be entered into the router before it will work. Many routers allow a computer to be attached to them so information can be entered.

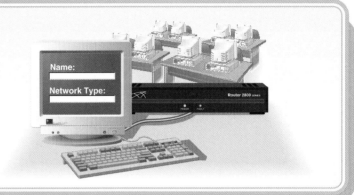

Speed

A router must analyze the information passing through it to determine the type of information and what action should be taken. Processing information can slow down a network if the router cannot process the information fast enough.

Most routers contain very fast processors to help prevent network slowdowns.

Repair Loops

In a large network, particularly a network that is not planned properly, the same information may continuously transfer, or loop, around the network. Routers prevent looping problems by analyzing the information they transfer and directing it to the proper destination.

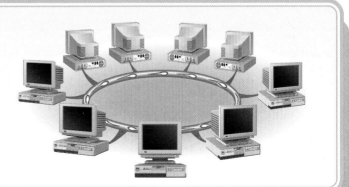

Router Types

Most routers can automatically determine the best route for information. With older routers, called static routers, a network administrator had to manually configure each route information could take. Newer routers, called dynamic routers, can automatically configure the available routes on the network.

Static Router   Dynamic Router

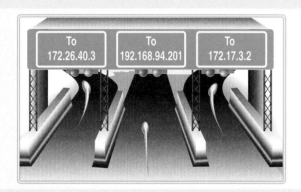

Addresses

Routers map networks and divide them into individual segments. Each segment is assigned a specific address. The network segment address and the address of the destination computer help the router determine the best route for the information to take through the network.

Formulas

Routers use mathematical formulas, called algorithms, to determine the best route that information should take. Routers use many variables, such as the distance and the speed of network segments, to determine which paths should be used to transfer information.

ROUTERS ON LARGE NETWORKS

Connect Different Network Types

Unlike some other types of network connectors, routers are often used to connect different types of networks together. Along with the ability to analyze the information and then determine the best route, routers can also translate the information into a form that can be transmitted on another type of network.

Protocols

A protocol is the language computers and devices use when communicating on a network. A router must understand the protocol being used to transmit information before it can route the information. Most routers understand the TCP/IP, IPX and AppleTalk protocols. Routers do not understand the NetBEUI or LAT protocols.

Wide Area Networks

Routers are often used to connect local area networks to a wide area network. Routers can also be used to break up the wide area network into segments. This helps reduce the amount of information being transferred over the network and improves the efficiency of the wide area network.

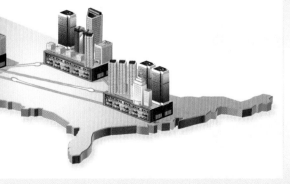

BROUTERS

A brouter is a connector that helps information transfer between networks. A brouter combines some of the characteristics of both a bridge and a router.

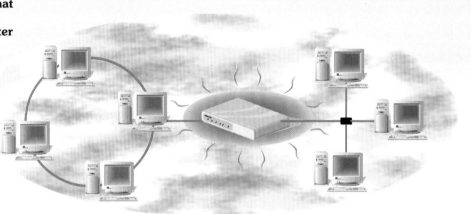

For information on bridges, see page 68. For information on routers, see page 70.

Route Information

When information passes through a brouter, the brouter first tries to determine the destination of the information by analyzing the protocol used to transfer the information.

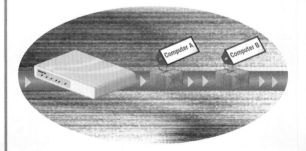

If the brouter can determine the destination of the information, the brouter then acts like a router and transfers the information along the best path.

Address

If a brouter cannot determine the destination of the information by studying the protocol, the brouter then tries to determine which network the destination computer is on.

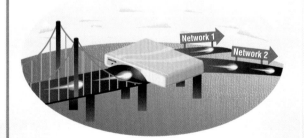

Once the destination network is determined, the brouter acts like a bridge and passes the information to the destination network.

GATEWAYS

A gateway is often used to link two different network types together. For example, you can use a gateway to transfer information between a Mac and a PC network.

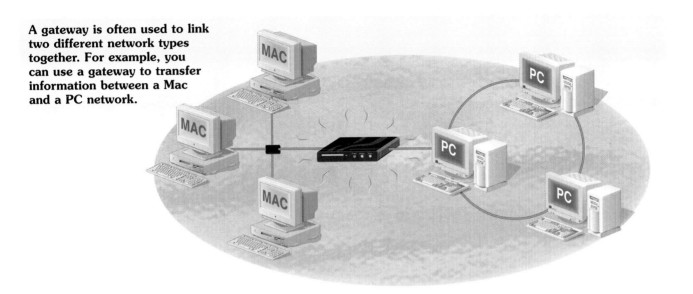

Hardware or Software

A gateway is used to pass information from one network to another. A gateway can be a hardware device that is physically connected to the network and transfers information between networks.

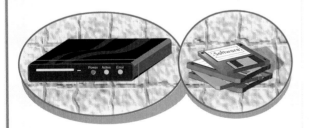

A gateway may also be software that allows two different protocols to exchange information on the same network.

Default Gateways

Information is forwarded to a default gateway if a network does not recognize the information's destination address.

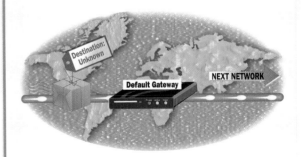

If the network does not know the destination address, the information is passed through the default gateway to the next network. Default gateways are most common on TCP/IP networks, such as the Internet.

MODEMS

Modems allow computers on a network to exchange information. A modem translates information into a form that can transmit over telephone lines. The receiving modem translates the information it receives into a form the computer can understand.

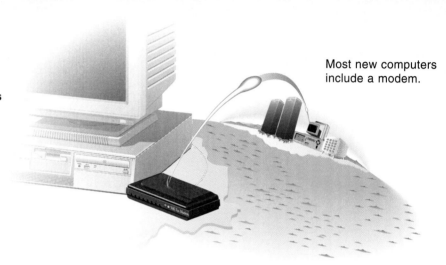

Most new computers include a modem.

Telephone Lines

Modems can use existing telephone lines to transfer information between networks. By using telephone lines, two computer devices can exchange information across vast distances.

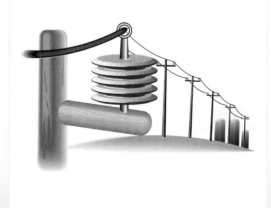

Wide Area Networks

Wide area networks (WANs) often have modems connecting areas of the network that transfer small amounts of information. Many companies use telephone lines to establish a permanent link between two modems in a wide area network.

Remote Access

Modems are commonly used to provide people with access to the company network while traveling. By using a modem to connect to the network, users are free to travel almost anywhere in the world and still access information on the network as well as communicate with other users.

Cost

Compared to other network devices, modems are an inexpensive way to communicate on a network. Since modems are inexpensive and easy to set up, they are a practical option for people who want to connect to the company network while away from the office.

Speed

Modems transfer information much slower than other network devices. For example, some network devices can transfer information as quickly as 10,000 kilobits per second (Kbs), while a fast modem may only transfer information at 50 kilobits per second (Kbs).

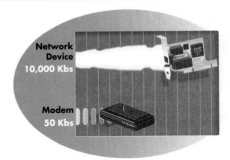

CHANNEL SERVICE NETWORK UNITS

Channel service network units are used to connect computer networks to public telephone networks.

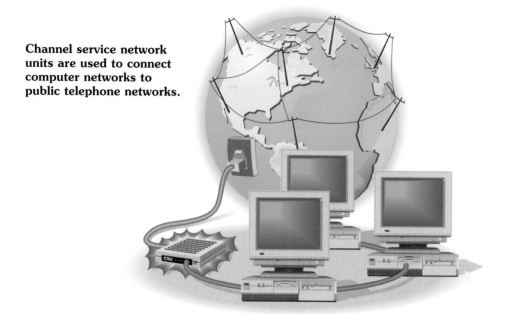

Public Telephone Networks

A public telephone network is similar to the regular telephone system. A public telephone network is usually run by a company that lets businesses lease a telephone line so they can transfer information from one city to another.

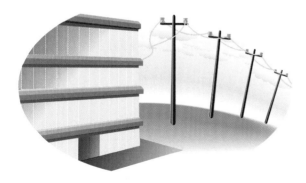

Data Conversion

Before information can be transferred, the information from a computer network may have to be converted into a form that will transfer over the public telephone network. A Channel Service Unit (CSU) is the device used to convert the information.

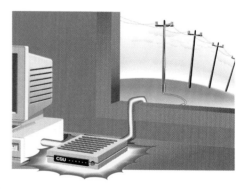

When the information reaches the other side of the connection, a Digital Service Unit (DSU) is used to convert the information back into a form that the computer can understand.

Multiplexers are network devices that are used to combine different types of information so they can transfer over a single transmission medium at the same time.

Information Types

Networks can transfer several different types of information, such as voice, video and computer data. Each type of information uses a different method to transfer over a network.

Combining Information

In many wide area networks, a single connection is used to connect different parts of the network. To transfer different types of information over the connection at the same time, the information must be combined into a single signal. A multiplexer is often used to combine different types of information into one signal and then transfer the combined signal over the connection.

When the combined signal reaches the other side of the connection, a multiplexer separates, or demultiplexes, the information again.

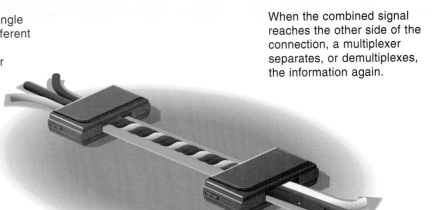

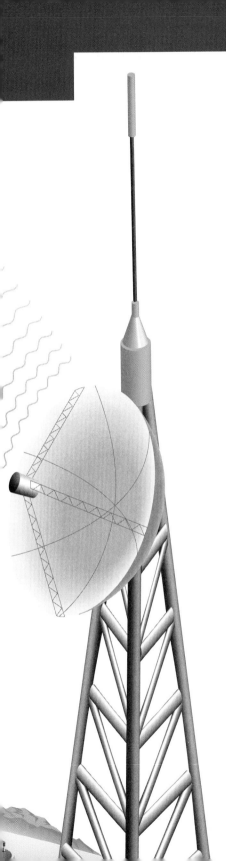

CHAPTER 4

Transmission Media

Transmission media is used to transfer information on a network. This chapter explains the difference between cable, light and wireless transmission media.

INTRODUCTION TO TRANSMISSION MEDIA

Transmission media are the physical pathways that connect computers and devices on a network.

Compatibility

A transmission medium allows two or more computers on a network to communicate. Each transmission medium requires specialized network hardware to transfer information. Network hardware, such as network interface cards, must be compatible with the type of transmission medium used.

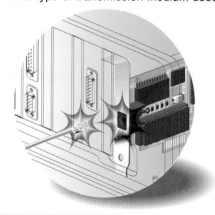

Combined Media

There are many different types of transmission media. Smaller networks are usually constructed using only one type of transmission medium. Larger networks may use different types of transmission media in various parts of the network.

Networks using a combination of transmission media are more complex and are difficult to build and maintain.

POPULAR TYPES OF TRANSMISSION MEDIA

Cable

Cable is the oldest and most commonly used type of transmission medium. Cable usually consists of copper wires covered with a protective plastic coating. Cable is inexpensive compared to other types of transmission media.

The three main types of cables are coaxial, unshielded twisted pair and shielded twisted pair.

Light

Many larger networks are now using light to transfer information. Fiber-optic cable transmits information by sending light signals through a core made of glass or plastic.

Networks using fiber-optic cable transfer information quickly, but they are expensive and difficult to install.

Wireless

A wireless network is often used when parts of a network cannot be physically connected. For example, a company may use wireless transmission media to connect office buildings that are on opposite sides of a lake.

Examples of wireless transmission media include infrared, radio, microwave and satellite systems.

TRANSMISSION MEDIA CONSIDERATIONS

There are many factors to consider before deciding which type of transmission medium is needed to build or expand a network.

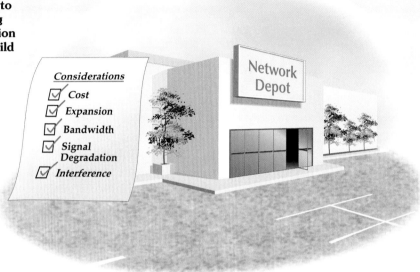

Considerations
- ☑ Cost
- ☑ Expansion
- ☑ Bandwidth
- ☑ Signal Degradation
- ☑ Interference

Network Depot

Cost

The price of transmission media plays an important role in determining how much it will cost to build a network. Transmission media range in price from a few cents per foot of cable to multi-million dollar satellite networks.

Expansion

As the needs of a company grow, the network may be expanded to accommodate new equipment or users. Since some types of network transmission media are difficult to alter after installation, it is important to consider the possibility of expansion before beginning to build the network.

For example, most cable-based networks are easy to manipulate, while fiber-optic networks are not.

Bandwidth

Bandwidth describes the amount of information that can be transferred at once using a specific transmission medium. The more information a transmission medium can transmit at once, the higher the bandwidth. Bandwidth is usually measured in megabits per second (Mbps).

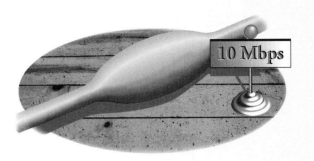

Signal Degradation

The further a signal has to travel along a transmission medium, the weaker the signal becomes. The weakening of the signal is called attenuation.

Each type of transmission medium can transmit signals a certain distance. The distance signals are required to travel may determine the type of transmission medium to use on the network.

Interference

Modern office buildings include many devices that may interfere with signals traveling along transmission media. Devices such as photocopiers, elevators and fluorescent lights may emit signals that could disrupt transmission media. Some types of transmission media are designed to better withstand interference.

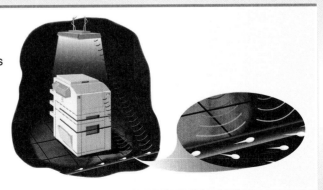

Coaxial cable is one of the most common types of transmission media used to create networks.

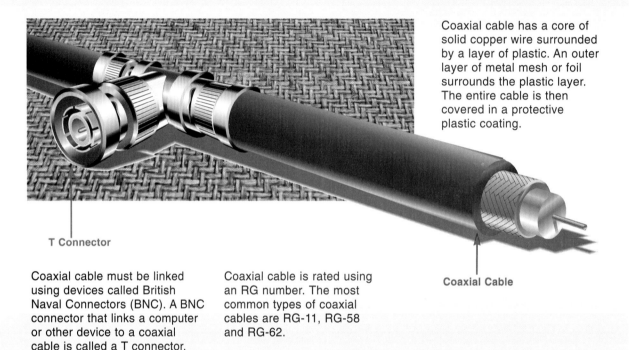

Coaxial cable has a core of solid copper wire surrounded by a layer of plastic. An outer layer of metal mesh or foil surrounds the plastic layer. The entire cable is then covered in a protective plastic coating.

T Connector

Coaxial Cable

Coaxial cable must be linked using devices called British Naval Connectors (BNC). A BNC connector that links a computer or other device to a coaxial cable is called a T connector.

Coaxial cable is rated using an RG number. The most common types of coaxial cables are RG-11, RG-58 and RG-62.

Interference

Coaxial cable transmits electrical signals through a network. Although the metal mesh or foil covering the cable protects the signals from interference, the electrical signals produced by nearby devices can affect the signals being transferred.

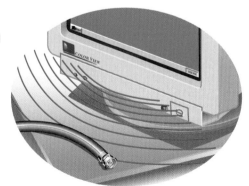

It is also possible for coaxial cable signals to interfere with other sensitive electrical devices in the area.

Electrical Resistance

Coaxial cable is rated by the amount of resistance the cable has to the transmission of electrical signals. Electrical resistance is measured in ohms. The most common rating of coaxial cable is 50 ohms.

Terminators

When coaxial cable is used on a bus network, there must be a terminator at each end of a cable to absorb the signals. A terminator must have the same electrical resistance rating as the cable. For example, a 50 ohm coaxial cable must use a 50 ohm resistor.

Bandwidth

Most coaxial networks transmit information at speeds of up to 10 megabits per second (Mbps), although thicker coaxial cable can transmit information much faster.

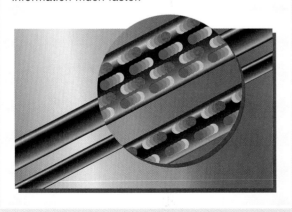

Cost

Coaxial cable is very inexpensive. It is widely used in networks because it has a lower price per foot than most other transmission media.

UNSHIELDED TWISTED PAIR CABLE

Unshielded Twisted Pair (UTP) cable is the most popular type of cable used to build new networks.

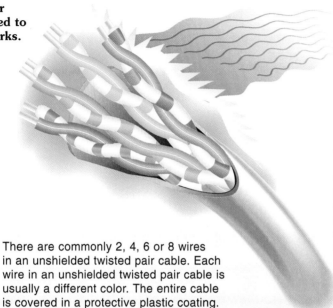

Unshielded twisted pair cable has a pair of copper wires that are twisted around each other. By twisting the wires around each other, the cable is less prone to interference from other electrical signals, such as the signals emitted by photocopiers or other nearby electrical equipment.

There are commonly 2, 4, 6 or 8 wires in an unshielded twisted pair cable. Each wire in an unshielded twisted pair cable is usually a different color. The entire cable is covered in a protective plastic coating.

Connectors

Unshielded twisted pair cables are connected using connectors similar to telephone jacks. These connectors are referred to as RJ-45 connectors.

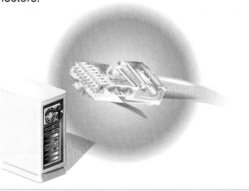

Cost

Unshielded twisted pair cable is the least expensive of all cable types.

Installation

Unshielded twisted pair cable is very lightweight and flexible compared to other cable types. These characteristics make unshielded twisted pair cable easy to install.

Except for very basic installations, qualified cable contractors should install all networking cable.

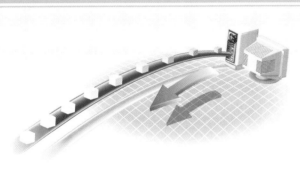

Cable Lengths

Unshielded twisted pair cable is not suitable for connecting devices that are far apart. The farther a signal must travel along a cable, the weaker the signal becomes. Unshielded twisted pair cable can reliably transmit information for up to a few hundred feet, but longer lengths may not transmit information properly.

Bandwidth

There are five main categories of unshielded twisted pair cables. Each category is capable of transmitting different amounts of information at once. Categories 1 and 2 can transfer up to 4 megabits per second (Mbps). Category 3 can transfer up to 16 Mbps. Category 4 can transfer up to 20 Mbps and Category 5 can transfer up to 100 Mbps.

SHIELDED TWISTED PAIR CABLE

Shielded Twisted Pair (STP) cable is similar to unshielded twisted pair cable, except that shielded twisted pair cable includes a protective metal or foil covering.

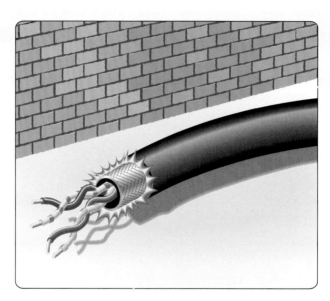

A shielded twisted pair cable can contain a single pair of wires or several pairs of wires.

Interference

Shielded twisted pair cable consists of pairs of twisted copper wires wrapped in a metal mesh or foil cover called a shield. The primary purpose of shielding a twisted pair cable is to protect the wires from interference from other electrical signals. The shield also prevents the cable from emitting its own electrical interference.

Bandwidth

Shielded twisted pair cable is capable of transmitting data at very high speeds of about 150 megabits per second (Mbps). Most networks that use shielded twisted pair cable rarely use speeds above 16 Mbps.

Maximum Speed
150 Mbps

Installation

It is sometimes difficult to install shielded twisted pair cable because it is bulky and not very flexible. One problem with shielded twisted pair cable is that it can be up to 0.5 inches in diameter. This can make installation awkward if a lot of cables need to be grouped together.

Connectors

Shielded twisted pair cable can use two types of connectors, depending on the network type. Apple LocalTalk networks use small pin and socket connectors, while IBM token-ring networks use bulky two-way connectors.

Both of these connectors are difficult to install. Cable can often be purchased with the connectors already attached.

Cost

Shielded twisted pair cable is more expensive than unshielded twisted pair cable, but is considered to be quite inexpensive compared to other types of transmission media.

FIBER-OPTIC CABLE

Fiber-optic cable uses light signals to transfer information through a network.

Fiber-optic cable transmits light signals through a core made of glass or plastic. The core is surrounded with gel or plastic to protect it from damage and signal loss. The cable is then covered with a plastic coating.

Cost

Fiber-optic cable and related equipment are very expensive to purchase and install. Fiber-optic cable is usually used as the main cable, or the backbone, of a network because of the high cost.

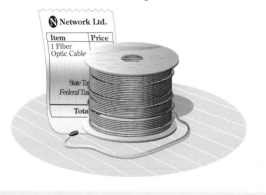

Service

Fiber-optic cable can be hard to work with and should only be installed and serviced by experienced technicians. Particular care should be given to glass core fiber-optic cable, which can break easily. Expensive monitoring equipment may be needed to locate a break in a fiber-optic cable.

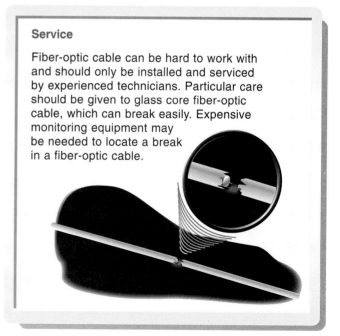

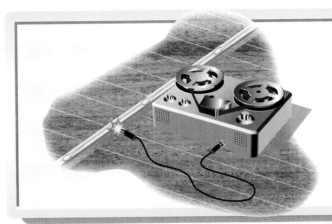

Interference

Fiber-optic cable does not emit electrical signals and is not susceptible to interference from other devices, such as photocopiers. Due to these factors, fiber-optic cable is ideal for companies concerned about security and electronic eavesdropping.

Signal Degradation

With many types of transmission media, the farther a signal travels over the medium, the weaker the signal becomes. Signals transmitted through fiber-optic cable are not greatly affected by attenuation. It is possible to transmit signals for many miles without any detectable degradation in the signal.

Bandwidth

Fiber-optic cable can transfer information at speeds of over 100 megabits per second (Mbps). Some types of fiber-optic cables are capable of transferring information at well over 2 gigabits per second (Gbps), but equipment that can utilize such a high rate of speed is not readily available.

INFRARED SYSTEMS

Infrared systems use infrared light to carry information between devices in a network. Infrared systems use the same technology as household remote controls.

Installation

The setup and installation of an infrared system is quite easy if it is used to connect devices on a local area network. Computers and equipment, such as printers, send infrared signals to a receiver attached to a central point on the ceiling. The receiver on the ceiling then beams the signal back down to all the devices. The devices must be positioned where they can easily send and receive infrared signals.

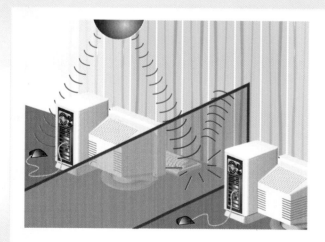

Interference

The biggest interference problem is usually caused by a physical barrier between two infrared devices, which disturbs the signal. This can be remedied by moving one of the devices to a better location.

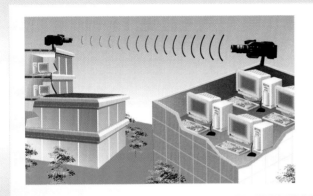

Signal Degradation

Infrared signals cannot travel very far without weakening significantly. Even with a clear line of sight between two devices, the signal may start to degrade if the distance is beyond the size of an office. If high-powered laser-based systems are used, infrared systems can be used over much longer distances.

Bandwidth

Infrared systems are not very fast. On a local area network, infrared devices can typically be used to transfer information at about 4 megabits per second (Mbps). Although well below the capabilities of wire cables, infrared systems may be suitable for networks that do not transfer a high volume of information.

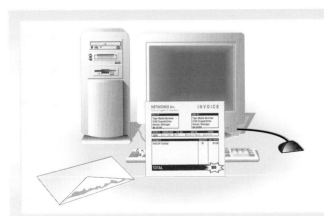

Cost

Infrared systems are more expensive than cable-based systems. Using infrared systems to transmit over long distances can be costly because of the high-powered transmitters that are required to generate the infrared signals.

RADIO SYSTEMS

Many companies are now using radio waves as a wireless transmission medium to connect devices on a network.

Radio systems can be used with any size of network. They are most often used to connect devices spread over a wide area, such as a city.

Radio Waves

Radio waves are often used as a wireless method of communicating between networks. Buildings have special transmitters and receivers positioned where they can easily exchange radio wave signals with networks in other buildings.

Mobility

Radio systems allow devices on a network to be more mobile. Many employees need to have access to the company network while they are away from the office. Radio systems are well suited for connecting portable computers to a network.

Interference

Radio systems transmit signals on radio frequencies. Radio systems are usually capable of detecting which frequencies are clear before starting to transmit information, so interference from other transmissions is usually not a problem.

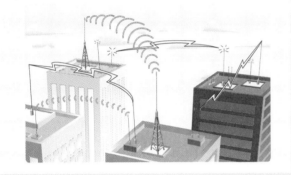

Bandwidth

Radio systems transmit less information at once than many types of cable-based networks.

Radio systems usually transmit information at speeds of up to 2 megabits per second (Mbps).

Service

Adding devices to a radio system is usually very simple. Installation often involves adding a radio device, such as a transmitter or receiver, to the computer.

Unlike most other types of transmission media, radio systems do not require cables or connectors to attach devices together.

Cost

Radio systems are relatively expensive when compared to cable-based networks. Some radio systems require the approval of a local communications authority before they can be used.

Microwave systems can be used to transfer information between networks in a wide area network.

Microwave systems are useful for connecting networks separated by an area where a physical connection is impossible, such as across a major highway or a lake.

Land-based Systems

Microwave transmissions can be used to transfer information when there is a clear line of sight between two locations.

It is possible to set up relay stations to create a microwave system that spans the length of a country. Relay stations are necessary to maintain the strength of the signal along the transmission path.

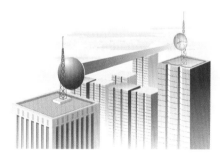

Land-based microwave stations can be recognized by the small parabolic dishes on telephone towers on top of buildings.

Interference

Microwave transmissions can be affected by environmental conditions such as smog or rain. Most microwave transmitting and receiving stations are designed to function under most environmental conditions.

Bandwidth

Microwave systems are capable of transferring large amounts of data compared to other types of wireless transmission media. The bandwidth of most land-based microwave systems is 10 megabits per second (Mbps).

Service

Microwave transmitter and receiver stations must be precisely aligned to efficiently transfer information. Microwave systems must be installed and maintained by properly trained and licensed service technicians. Almost all microwave installations are subject to the regulations of a governing body, such as the FCC (Federal Communications Commission) in the United States.

Cost

Microwave systems are costly to install but in many cases they are the only option for creating a connection between two locations that are separated by a great distance, such as two cities.

SATELLITE SYSTEMS

Satellite systems use satellites orbiting at approximately 22,300 miles above the Earth to relay signals from one part of a wide area network to another.

Satellite systems are also ideal for communicating with remote areas, such as ships at sea.

Installation

The setup and installation of a satellite system often involves many different companies. Satellite system installations must be completed by firms and service technicians who are governed by a regulation body similar to the FCC (Federal Communications Commission) in the United States.

Cost

Satellite systems are very expensive. The cost of building, launching and maintaining a satellite system is usually shared by many companies who then share the available bandwidth of the system. A new satellite system often costs well over a billion dollars to set up.

Delays

Each time a signal is transferred over a satellite system, the signal travels 22,300 miles up to the satellite and then travels back to the receiving system on Earth. This can cause delays in transferring from 0.5 to 5 seconds.

The distance a signal travels across the Earth does not have a great effect on the delay. Sending a signal to another part of the state by satellite takes approximately the same amount of time as sending a signal to the other side of the country.

Interference

Transmissions between the Earth system and a satellite may be affected by interference caused by weather and atmospheric conditions.

Most satellite systems are designed to compensate for any interference from common weather conditions, such as rain or fog.

Bandwidth

Very high bandwidths are available for satellite systems. The higher the bandwidth in a satellite system, the higher the cost.

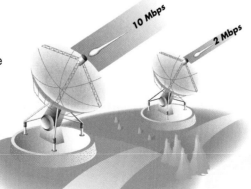

Most companies use a bandwidth of between 2 and 10 megabits per second (Mbps).

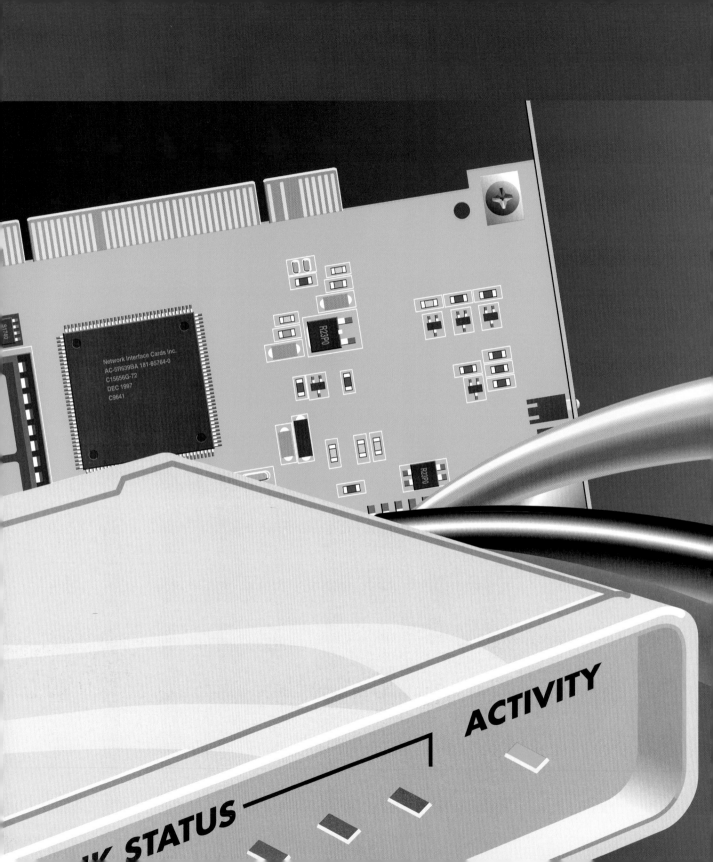

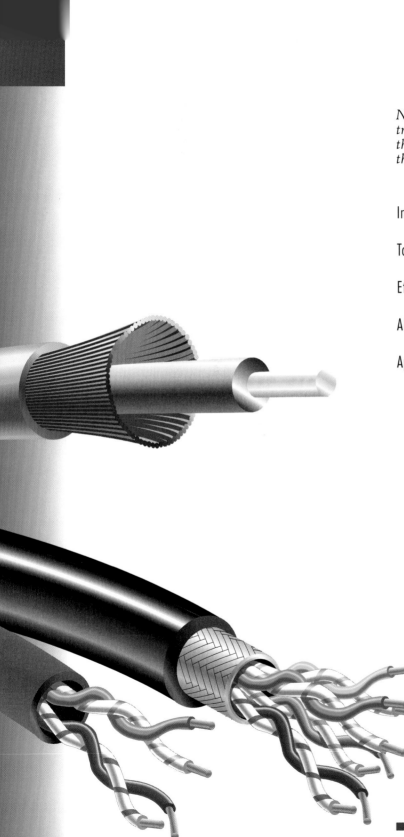

Network Architecture

Network architecture defines how information transfers on a network. This chapter discusses the three main types of network architectures that you will find in networks around the world.

INTRODUCTION TO NETWORK ARCHITECTURE

Network architecture refers to how information transfers on a network.

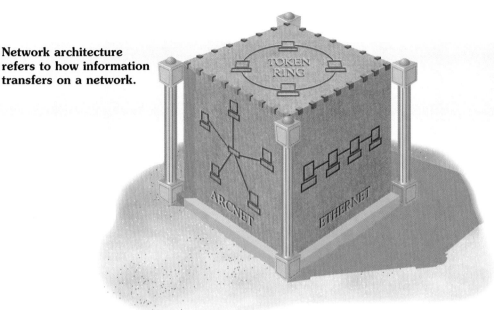

The three main types of network architectures are Token Ring, ARCnet and Ethernet.

Network Architecture

Network architecture defines how the computers and devices on a network transfer information through transmission media. Network architecture also determines how information transfers through the network structure, such as the bus, ring or star structure.

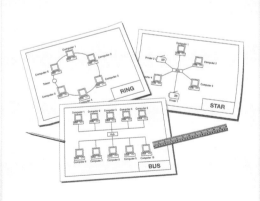

Network Standards

All of the components of a network, such as hardware, software and transmission media, are designed to work with a specific type of network architecture.

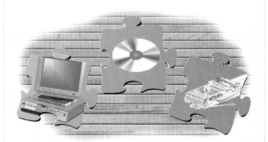

Network standards ensure that all of a network's components can work together. A device designed for one type of network architecture cannot be used on another type of network.

ARCHITECTURE CONSIDERATIONS

Information Transfer

The amount of information transferred at once, called bandwidth, varies for each network architecture. As the bandwidth increases, the network becomes more complex. The type of information that is transferred is another factor to consider.

For example, one architecture may be suited to transfer large files such as images, while another architecture may be better at transferring small files such as word processing documents.

Network Size

Many networks can be purchased as a single kit that will connect a small number of computers. Large networks are often complex and must be installed by trained professionals.

Since some architectures restrict the maximum number of computers and devices on a single segment of the network, the size of the network may affect which architecture is used.

Cost

Each architecture has different requirements for installation, maintenance and expansion. These differences affect the overall cost of the network. An efficient, reliable network that can transfer information quickly is usually more expensive.

TOKEN RING ARCHITECTURE

Token Ring architecture was developed by IBM in 1984. Token Ring is no longer a popular choice for new network installations.

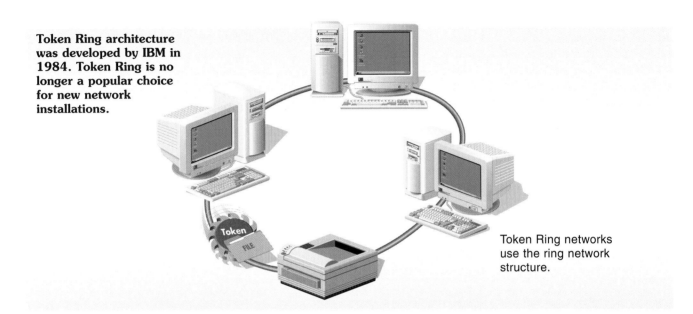

Token Ring networks use the ring network structure.

Tokens

A token is a signal that regulates the flow of information on a network. Token Ring networks work by passing a single token from computer to computer. Before a computer can send information, it must collect the token. This ensures only one computer can transmit information at a time.

Bandwidth

Token Ring networks can operate at different speeds. The speed is determined by the type of cable used on the network. Token Ring networks can transfer information at either 4 megabits per second (Mbps) using unshielded twisted pair cables or 16 Mbps using shielded twisted pair cables.

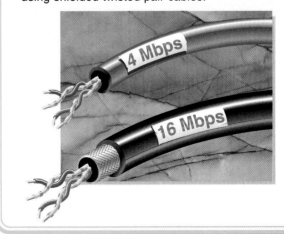

Cables

Shielded and unshielded twisted pair cables are the most common transmission media used in Token Ring networks. Many Token Ring networks are now using fiber-optic cable.

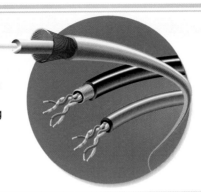

With fiber-optic cable, Token Ring networks are capable of transferring data at very high speeds.

Troubleshooting

The token travels in one direction around the network, so it is easy to determine the location of a problem or break in the network.

If the token cannot pass beyond a certain point, the token can travel in the opposite direction until it encounters the error again. This helps to pinpoint the location of an error in the network.

Cost

Token Ring networks are more expensive than other types of cable-based networks. This is one reason Token Ring networks are becoming less popular and are being replaced by other types of network architectures.

ETHERNET ARCHITECTURE

Ethernet is the most popular architecture used when building new networks.

The Ethernet architecture has been widely accepted as a network standard since the early 1980s.

Compatibility

Since Ethernet is so popular and widely accepted, most manufacturers of network software and devices, such as network printers, ensure that their products will work when used on an Ethernet network.

The most common operating standards for Ethernet networks are defined by the Institute of Electrical and Electronic Engineers (IEEE).

Information Transfer

Unlike other network architectures, Ethernet does not use a token to transfer information on the network. To send information, each computer on an Ethernet network waits for a pause on the network.

If two computers send information at the same time, a collision occurs and the computers must try again to send the information.

Cost

One of the many reasons Ethernet is the most popular network architecture is because it is relatively inexpensive when compared to other network architectures.

The Ethernet cards used in most personal computers can be purchased for less than 50 dollars and can be connected using cable that costs only pennies per foot.

Bandwidth

Ethernet networks can transfer information at different speeds, depending on the type of Ethernet network used.

The most common type of Ethernet network used in offices can transfer information at 10 megabits per second (Mbps).

Fast/Gigabit Ethernet

Newer Ethernet networks can now transfer information at speeds of 100 megabits per second (Mbps) and faster. Fast and Gigabit Ethernet wire was developed to efficiently transfer more complex types of information, such as videos and images.

ETHERNET ARCHITECTURE

Ethernet networks require specific types of cables to transfer information.

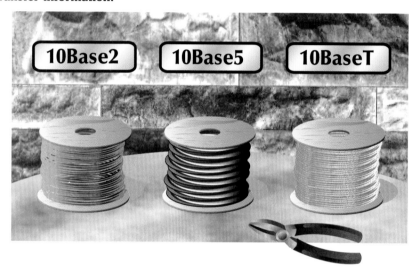

Ethernet networks use a system of numbers and words to specify the type of cable needed to build the network. Each type of cable can transmit different amounts of information over varying distances.

It is important to use the correct type of cable for the network. If a company installs or upgrades a network, cable suppliers can help choose the type of Ethernet cable needed.

10Base2

10Base2 cable is often found in smaller networks using the bus network structure. For instance, a small department in a company could connect computers using 10Base2 cable. 10Base2 is a type of coaxial cable that resembles the cable a TV company uses to transmit signals into houses. 10Base2 cable is also referred to as thinnet.

10Base2 cable can transfer information at speeds of up to 10 megabits per second (Mbps). Each cable in a 10Base2 network must not exceed 607 feet.

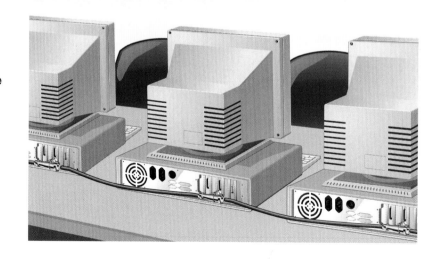

10Base5

10Base5 cable is not often used in new network installations. 10Base5 cable is a coaxial cable that is thick and inflexible. The thickness of the cable makes it difficult to set up and install. 10Base5 cable is also referred to as thicknet.

10Base5 cable can transfer information at speeds of up to 10 megabits per second (Mbps). Each cable in a 10Base5 network must not exceed 1,640 feet.

10Base5 cables usually have transceivers attached to them. The transceiver translates information so the Ethernet cable can exchange information with the network interface card in the computer.

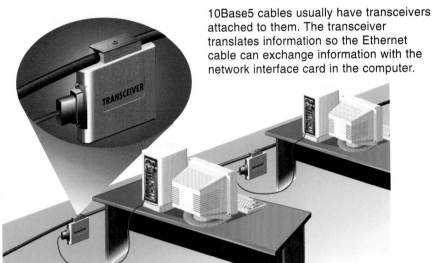

10BaseT

10BaseT cable is most often used to build new Ethernet networks. 10BaseT is relatively inexpensive and is easy to install and service. A cable connecting a computer to a network hub must not exceed 328 feet.

10BaseT uses unshielded twisted pair cable that can transfer information at speeds of 10 or 100 megabits per second (Mbps). Twisted pair cable that can transfer information at 100 Mbps is also called 100BaseT.

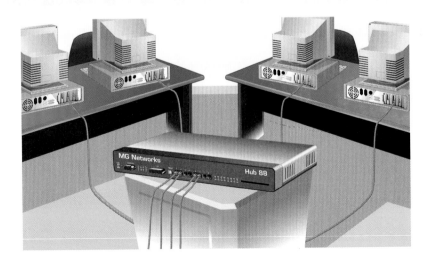

INFORMATION TRANSFER

Ethernet networks have different methods of specifying the way information is sent and received on a network.

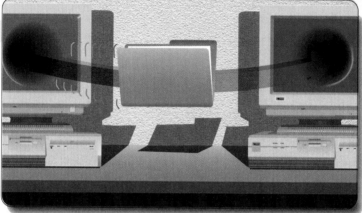

Access methods ensure that the information is safely transmitted. When two or more devices on an Ethernet network transmit information at the same time, a collision occurs. The information must then be retransmitted.

ACCESS METHODS

CSMA/CD

Carrier Sense Multiple Access with Collision Detection (CSMA/CD) is the most popular method of controlling the transfer of information on an Ethernet network. This method is very effective when used on Ethernet networks that have large numbers of users.

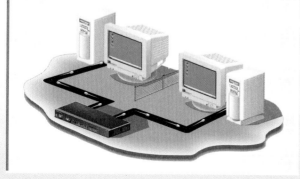

CSMA/CA

Carrier Sense Multiple Access with Collision Avoidance (CSMA/CA) is a second method of controlling the transfer of information on an Ethernet network. CSMA/CA is also the access method used in AppleTalk networks.

Multiple Access

Multiple access means that many computers and other network devices can attempt to send data on the network at the same time.

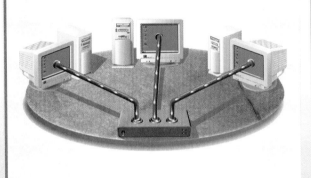

Carrier Sense

When a device transmits information on a network, it monitors the network to see if other devices are transmitting information. If the device detects another signal, called a carrier, the device stops transmitting information, pauses and then begins transmitting the information again.

Collision Detection

After a device sends information on an Ethernet network, it checks the network transmission medium to make sure the information has not collided with any other information. If the device detects a collision, it pauses and then tries to resend the information.

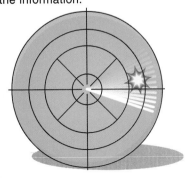

Collision Avoidance

An Ethernet device can avoid collisions by letting other devices know when it is about to transmit information. All the other network devices then refrain from using the network.

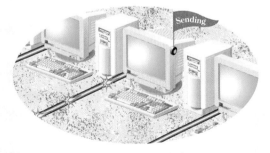

Since each device is informed about every transmission on the network, this method of access control can be very inefficient.

ARCNET ARCHITECTURE

ARCnet is one of the oldest types of network architectures used for personal computers. ARCnet networks are often simple, inexpensive and flexible.

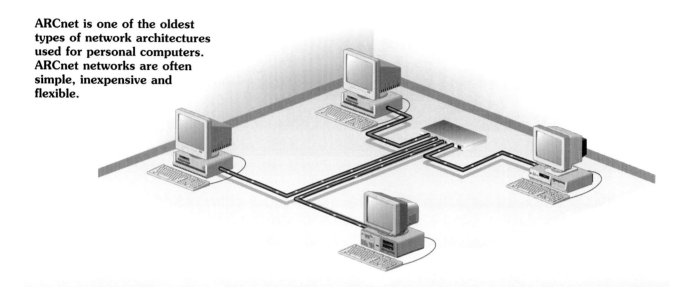

Tokens

Like the Token Ring architecture, ARCnet uses a token to control the flow of information on the network. A computer on the network must collect the token before it can transmit information. The computers on an ARCnet network are numbered in sequence and the token is passed to each one in order.

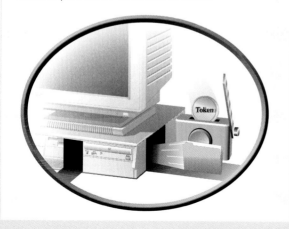

Hubs

The hub is the center of the ARCnet network. Each ARCnet network uses a star network structure to connect the computers.

There are three types of ARCnet hubs. Passive hubs simply connect the cable segments together. Active hubs contain electronic components that reproduce the signal as it passes from segment to segment, preventing errors and interference. Smart hubs can perform routine tasks such as error detection and allow network administrators to have more control over each network segment.

Availability

Although the ARCnet architecture is not popular in new networks, there are still many existing ARCnet networks. ARCnet has always been relatively inexpensive and has been available for 30 years.

Many companies that have older, smaller networks use ARCnet.

Bandwidth

An ARCnet network can transfer information at a speed of about 2.5 megabits per second (Mbps). Newer versions of ARCnet, known as ARCnet Plus, can transfer data at speeds of up to 20 Mbps. ARCnet networks commonly use coaxial cable as the transmission medium.

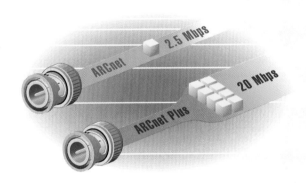

Efficient

Although ARCnet has a low bandwidth, it is an efficient method of transferring information when compared to other network architectures. ARCnet does little processing of the information that is transferring over the network, and is often used in networks that gather information, such as in a manufacturing plant or a laboratory.

APPLE NETWORKS

Apple developed the AppleTalk architecture to control the transfer of information on networks with Apple computers.

The AppleTalk architecture is built into the Macintosh operating system. Each computer using the Macintosh operating system has networking capabilities.

A later version of AppleTalk is called AppleTalk Phase2. AppleTalk networks are also often referred to as LocalTalk networks.

LocalTalk

LocalTalk refers to the network hardware on an AppleTalk network. Macintosh computers have built-in LocalTalk network hardware, such as connectors and interface cards.

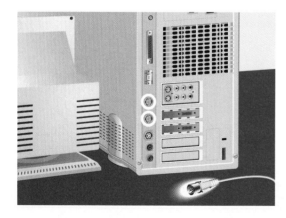

Zones

LocalTalk networks are made up of small networks or workgroups, called zones. Each zone can contain a maximum of 32 computers.

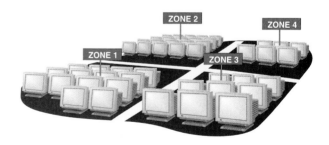

Several zones can be connected to form a single, larger network, called an internetwork. Computers on the internetwork can then access the resources located in other zones.

AppleShare Servers

LocalTalk networks use file and print servers called AppleShare servers. Each Macintosh computer has built-in software that allows the user to access the AppleShare servers on the network.

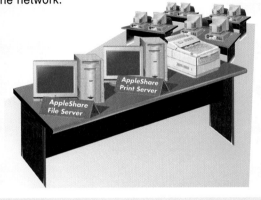

Cost

LocalTalk networks are less expensive to set up than other types of network architectures because much of the required software and hardware are already part of the Macintosh computers.

Transfer Information

The cable used for LocalTalk networks is usually shielded twisted pair, although standard telephone cable can also be used.

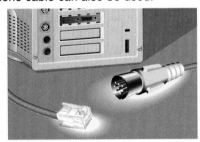

LocalTalk networks can only transfer information at speeds of up to 0.22 megabits per second (Mbps). This slow transfer speed often discourages large companies from using LocalTalk networks.

EtherTalk

An EtherTalk card is an interface card that allows an Apple computer to connect to an Ethernet network. Ethernet networks can transfer information much faster and more efficiently than a LocalTalk network.

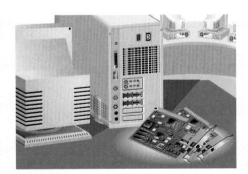

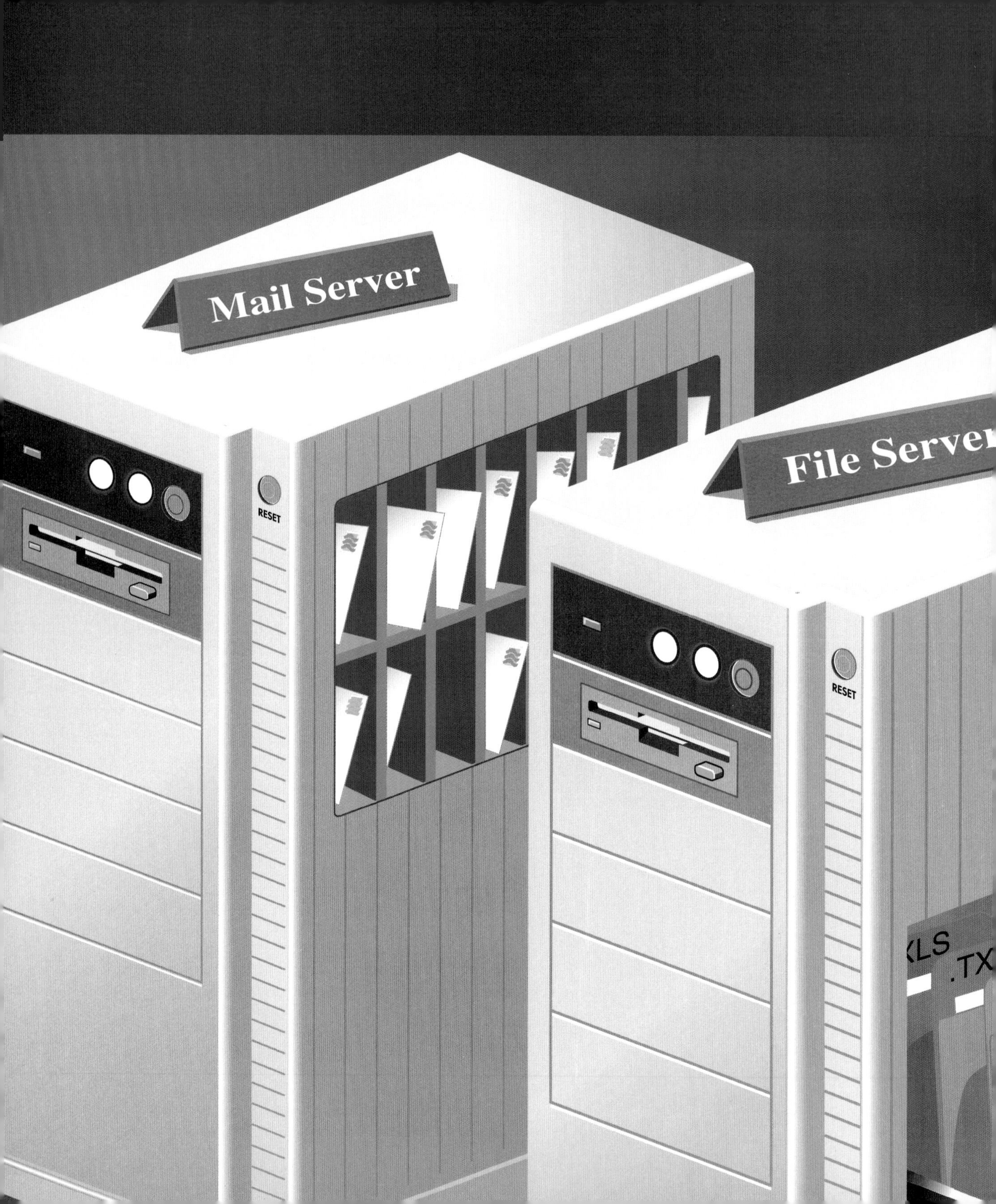
Mail Server
RESET
File Server
RESET
XLS
.TX

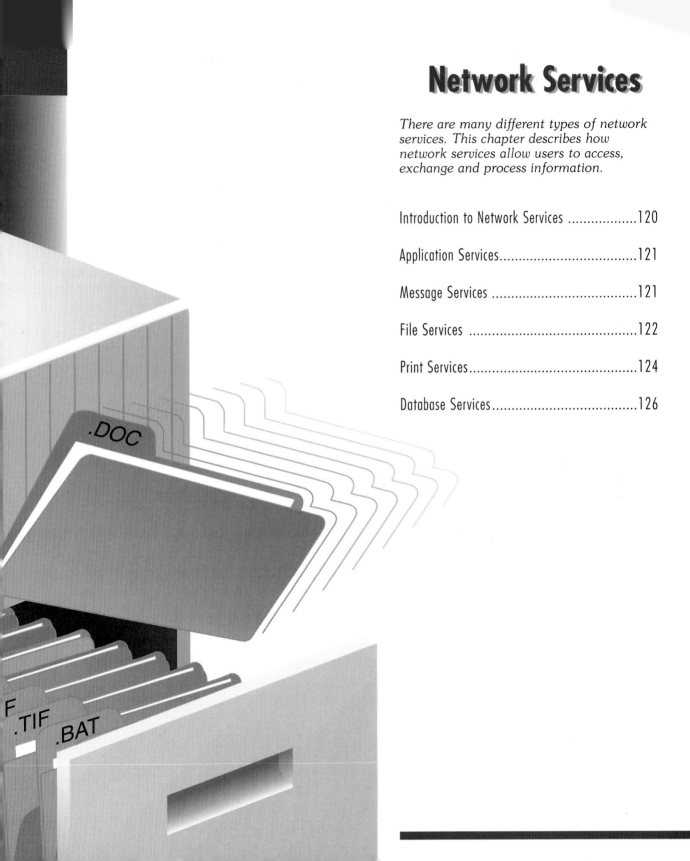

Network Services

There are many different types of network services. This chapter describes how network services allow users to access, exchange and process information.

INTRODUCTION TO NETWORK SERVICES

Network services allow users to share and access information and resources on a network.

Services

There are many types of services available for networks. Each type of service is responsible for performing a specific task. The most common types of services help users exchange files and information or use a network printer. Most network operating systems include several types of services.

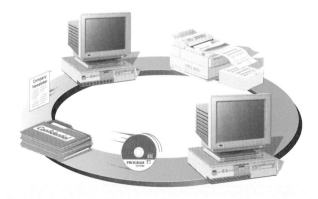

Servers

Network services are usually organized, managed and run on servers. Servers are powerful computers that have a lot of memory and processing power. Most servers on a network are kept in a central location to make managing the servers easier. Network servers are very expensive to buy and maintain. Most servers on a network operate continuously.

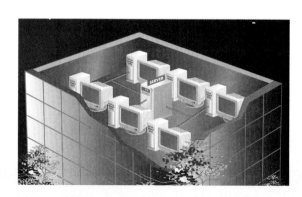

APPLICATION SERVICES

An application service is dedicated to running a program, or application, that anyone on the network can use.

Many application services are used for programs that require a lot of processing power, such as Computer Aided Design (CAD) programs. The client computers on a network do not need to have a lot of memory or processing power because the powerful application server runs the program.

MESSAGE SERVICES

Message services allow people to exchange electronic mail.

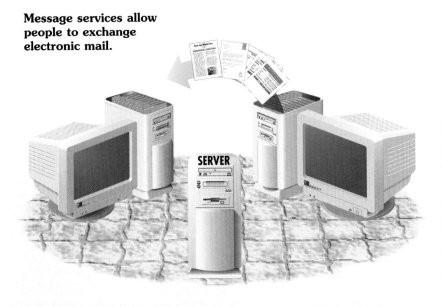

E-mail enables people in a company to exchange information quickly. Many message services offer several features, including the ability to confirm that a message sent on the network was received and the ability to send messages to people on the Internet. Message services allow users to exchange many different types of information, such as word processing documents, spreadsheets, video files and sound files.

FILE SERVICES

File services are used to store files on a file server. The information on a file server is secure, organized and can be accessed quickly.

Storage

The primary function of file services is to allow users to access files on a network. File services can let computers connected to the network retrieve and store files on the file server's hard drive or retrieve information from other storage devices on the server, such as a CD or optical drive.

Convenience

It is easy to store information on a server that offers file services. When a user saves files on a file server, it often appears as if the user's computer is saving the files to its own hard drive. Making storage space on a file server appear as the hard drive on a user's computer is known as mapping.

Sharing

File sharing is one of the most valuable uses of a network because it allows people to work together. For example, a company's marketing department can store its information on the file server so the latest information can be easily accessed by the sales department.

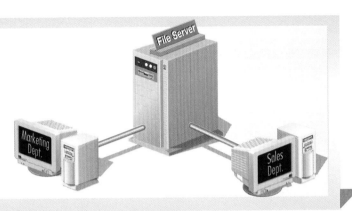

Security

Most file servers have very elaborate security systems to prevent unauthorized access or the accidental destruction of files stored on the server. Individual files on a file server may be restricted to a specific user or group of users.

Backup

Important files used on a network may be stored on a file server. Having important files stored in one location makes it easy to back up the data in case of a system failure.

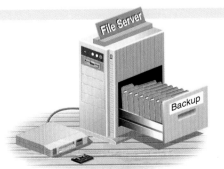

Most backup devices, such as a tape drive, can be connected directly to the file server.

PRINT SERVICES

Print services allow users on a network to share the same printer. On many networks, the print server is directly connected to the printer.

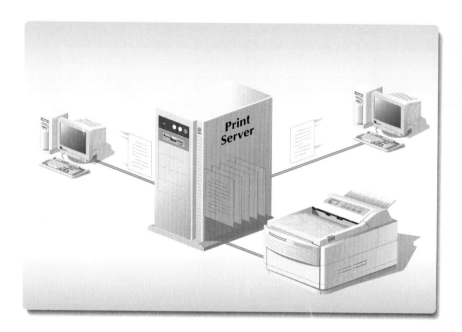

Spooling

Since many users can send documents to the same printer, the printer may become overloaded. A print server can temporarily store print jobs until the printer is available. This is called spooling. When the print server stores the print job, the user's computer is free to perform other tasks.

Control

Many print services allow users to control printer functions. Instead of having to manually change the settings on the printer, such as paper size or contrast, users may be able to adjust the settings from their own computers. Print services may also allow users to schedule their print jobs for times when the printer is not busy, such as at night or lunch time.

Cost-Effective

Using a print service to share a printer eliminates the need to buy a printer for each user on the network. Print services also make using expensive printing equipment, such as a color laser printer or a plotter, more cost-effective since the company only needs to buy one device that all users can share.

Remote Access

Network users may send information to the printer, regardless of the distance between their computers and the printer. For example, a person in the sales department may be able to print an order in the warehouse across the street if the person's computer and the printer are on the same network.

Fax

A print service may also be used to allow users to access a fax machine on the network. This allows many users to share a single machine. On large networks, fax machines are often connected to specialized fax servers.

DATABASE SERVICES

Database services help people on a network manage and work with large amounts of information. Database services are one of the most common types of services found on corporate networks.

Database Servers

A database server is used to manipulate information in a database and perform tasks that have been requested by clients, such as finding information in the database. A database server can handle requests from several clients at once. Most database servers are very powerful computers that require a lot of maintenance.

Clients

A client computer is used to request information from the database server. Client computers rarely process information from the database, which leaves the client computers free to perform other tasks. Client computers need much less processing power than a database server.

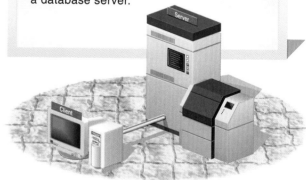

Distribution

Many database services store and process specific information on database servers in different geographic locations. This is called distributed computing.

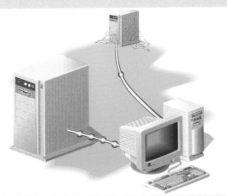

For example, a company may store frequently-accessed information locally and low-priority information on a server some distance away. Distribution helps make the processing of information more efficient and reliable.

Security

Most databases consist of information that may be restricted, such as a company's sales or payroll information. Database security is one of the primary concerns of a database service.

The database server is often located in a locked room and is only accessible to the network administrator.

SQL

Database services use a series of instructions called structured query language (SQL) to access and work with information in the database.

SQL is the most widely-used language for database services.

CHAPTER 7

Network Operating Systems

The software used to control the activity of a network is called a network operating system. This chapter discusses many types of network operating systems, such as Windows 95, NetWare, Unix and more.

NETWORK OPERATING SYSTEMS

A network operating system is the software used to control the overall activity of a network.

Powerful

Network operating systems are powerful programs that are capable of quickly processing large amounts of information. Many network operating systems are complex and should be installed and set up by qualified professionals.

Servers

Many networks use computers, called servers, to run the network operating system. A network operating system may run on multiple servers, each performing a specific task.

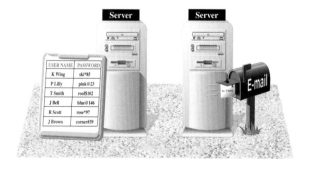

For example, one server may be used to control the user names and passwords of each user on the network. Another server may be used to allow users on the network to exchange e-mail messages.

Organize Resources

A network may use many resources, such as fax modems, printers and software applications. A network operating system organizes the resources on a network and ensures that all the parts of the network work together smoothly and efficiently.

Control Access

Many network operating systems have sophisticated security features to control access to information and devices on the network.

For example, a network operating system can ensure that only authorized people with a password can use the information stored on the network.

Operating System Drivers

An operating system driver is software that allows the computers on a network to communicate with the network operating system. A computer must have the appropriate drivers to access the network.

When a user performs a task, the driver determines whether the user's computer needs to access the network to complete the task.

WINDOWS FOR WORKGROUPS

Windows for Workgroups is the networking version of the Windows 3.1 operating system.

DOS-based Operating System

Windows for Workgroups is a Graphical User Interface (GUI, pronounced "gooey") that runs on computers using the DOS operating system. Since Windows for Workgroups requires DOS to run, Windows is not considered a true operating system.

16-bit Operating System

Operating systems are often identified by the amount of information they can process at once. Windows for Workgroups can process 16 bits of data at one time. A 16-bit operating system cannot run programs designed for an operating system that can process more information at once.

Most new operating systems, such as Windows NT, are 32-bit operating systems.

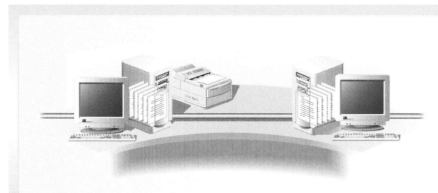

Sharing Resources

Windows for Workgroups operates on peer-to-peer based networks. Each user on the network can access other computers on the network. Users can also make resources on their computers, such as files and printers, available to other users.

Workgroups

A workgroup is a group of computers on a network that frequently access the same resources. Using workgroups makes it easy to administrate network resources. Instead of assigning passwords and login names to resources for each individual user on a network, an administrator can adjust the settings for an entire workgroup and apply them to all members of the workgroup.

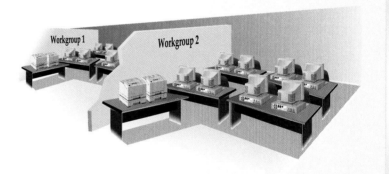

Built-in Features

Windows for Workgroups comes with several built-in features, such as e-mail and scheduling capabilities. These features help users and network administrators effectively work together on the network.

WINDOWS 95

Windows 95 is a graphical, easy-to-use operating system. Although Windows 95 is often found on personal computers, many companies use it as a network operating system.

Peer-to-peer

The Windows 95 operating system can operate on a peer-to-peer network. Each computer that runs Windows 95 can exchange information and resources with other Windows 95 computers on the network.

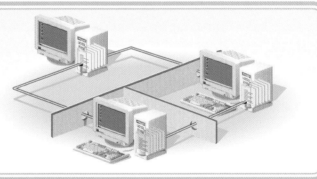

Cost

Using Windows 95 as a network operating system is an inexpensive way to build a network. Costs are reduced because the network does not require dedicated servers, such as file or print servers, or any additional software to connect the computers.

Popular

Windows 95 is one of the most popular operating systems in the world. There are an estimated 60 million computers using the Windows 95 operating system.

Due to the popularity of Windows 95, many networking products, such as network interface cards, are specifically designed to work with Windows 95.

Applications

Many applications have been developed to run on computers using Windows 95. Since Windows 95 is often used as a network operating system, most network administration packages are compatible with Windows 95.

Ease of Use

Windows 95 is very easy to use. Once the operating system is installed and the network has been set up, minimal training is required to teach users to exchange information over the network.

In many instances, a user may not even realize that Windows 95 is performing a task on the network.

WINDOWS NT

Microsoft Windows NT
is a powerful network
operating system.
Windows NT is available
in two main versions.

Windows NT Server

Windows NT Server is found on client/server
networks and has been optimized to support
the heavy processing demands of a dedicated
network server. The client computers on a
network running Windows NT Server can
use a variety of operating systems.

Windows NT Workstation

Windows NT Workstation is another version
of the Windows NT operating system and
is used most frequently on peer-to-peer
networks.

Windows NT Workstation can run most
applications that were designed to work
on earlier versions of the Windows
operating system.

32-bit Operating Systems

Both main versions of Windows NT are 32-bit operating systems. 32-bit refers to the amount of data processed at one time by the operating system. 32-bit operating systems effectively use the processing power of modern microprocessors such as the Intel Pentium® and Digital Alpha.

Ease of Use

The Windows NT operating system is very easy to use. Windows NT uses a Graphical User Interface (GUI, pronounced "gooey") to communicate with the user.

Many administrative tasks are made easier by using graphics instead of plain text to display information. Windows NT has the same look and feel as the Windows 95 operating system.

Support

There are many books and software applications, as well as technical support, available for people who use the Windows NT operating system.

Microsoft has designed courses to certify people who use and maintain the Windows NT operating system.

NetWare is an operating system developed by Novell for client/server networks.

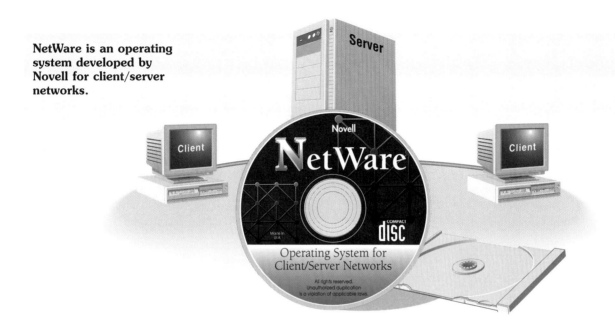

Number of Connections

NetWare is available in different versions. Each version allows a limited number of computers to connect to the NetWare server at one time. The cost increases with the number of connections allowed in each version.

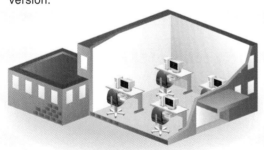

Before purchasing the NetWare operating system, make sure the version provides the number of connections needed.

Modules

The capabilities of a NetWare server can be increased by adding modules. Modules are add-on programs that provide additional features and work as part of the network operating system. Popular modules include programs that let people back up information on the network or monitor an uninterruptible power supply.

Support

NetWare is a well supported network operating system. Books, software applications and technical support are widely available for people who use NetWare.

Novell has also designed courses for people who plan to use and maintain the NetWare operating system.

Hardware

NetWare is one of the most widely used network operating systems in the world.

Since so many companies use the NetWare operating system, computer hardware, such as network interface cards and printers, is often designed so the hardware will function efficiently on a network running NetWare.

NetWare Lite

Novell also makes a network operating system for peer-to-peer networks, called NetWare Lite.

NetWare Lite has little in common with NetWare and is not widely used.

LANTASTIC

LANtastic is a network operating system that is well established and is often found in small to medium-sized companies.

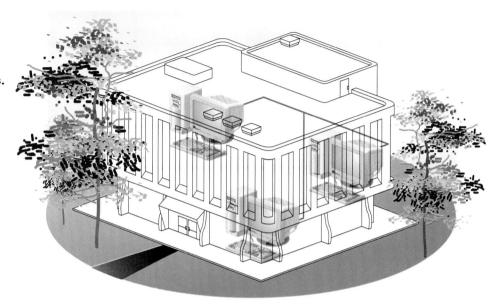

Peer-to-peer

LANtastic is found on peer-to-peer networks. Users can make files and resources on their computers, such as a printer, available to other computers on the network. Users can access the shared files and resources on the network.

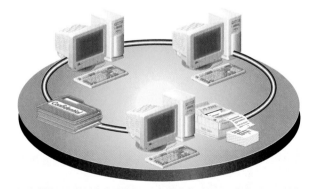

Versatile

The LANtastic operating system makes it easy to connect a group of computers that use a variety of operating systems. For example, LANtastic can allow computers using MS-DOS or Windows 3.1 to access information stored on computers using Windows 95. LANtastic also makes it easy to expand a network and add features later.

Additional Features

LANtastic offers improved and additional features that are not found on many network operating systems.

For example, LANtastic can connect Windows 95 computers as a network. Although Windows 95 has basic peer-to-peer networking functions built in, LANtastic offers improved networking features, such as better device sharing and electronic mail.

Modem Sharing

LANtastic allows users to share a modem on a network.

Instead of equipping each computer with a modem, all the users on a LANtastic network can share one modem.

Cost

LANtastic is inexpensive compared to other network operating systems. Unlike many other network operating systems, LANtastic is already equipped with features that make the network versatile and easy to expand. These benefits can make a LANtastic network up to 80% less expensive.

UNIX is an older, powerful operating system that can be used to run an entire network or a single user's computer.

Versions

UNIX is the oldest computer operating system still in widespread use today. Since its development in the late 1960s, many companies have owned UNIX. There are several versions of the UNIX operating system available.

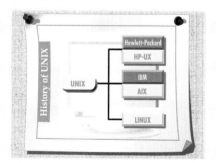

Hewlett-Packard makes a UNIX operating system called HP-UX. IBM's UNIX operating system is called AIX. Linux is a free version of UNIX available on the World Wide Web at http://www.linux.org

Power

The UNIX operating system is very powerful. UNIX is harder to install and set up than most other operating systems, but UNIX provides greater control over the computer's resources and power. As a result, a computer's performance may be significantly improved when running the UNIX operating system.

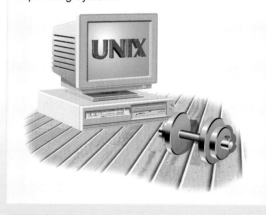

Multitasking

UNIX was originally developed to be the operating system for a single large computer called a mainframe computer. Since multiple users can access a mainframe computer at the same time, UNIX was developed to run many programs and perform numerous tasks at once, called multitasking.

UNIX's multitasking capabilities make it an efficient network operating system.

Security

UNIX has many built-in security features to protect information from accidental deletion or access by unauthorized users.

UNIX's security features are one of the reasons UNIX is such a popular operating system on the world's largest network, the Internet.

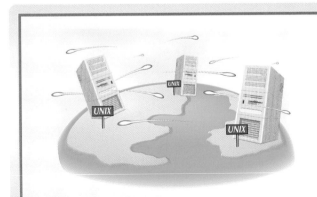

Internet

Many of the first computers used to establish the Internet ran the UNIX operating system. Even today, UNIX is the most widely used operating system for servers on the Internet.

CHAPTER 8

The OSI Model and Protocols

The OSI model is used to specify how computer networking devices should communicate with each other. This chapter discusses the OSI model as well as protocols, such as TCP/IP, IPX/SPX and NetBEUI.

The Open Systems Interconnection (OSI) model is used to specify how computer networking devices should communicate with each other.

Standards

Many products, often manufactured by different companies, are needed to create and maintain a network. Before a network can function properly, all the products on the network must be able to communicate with each other.

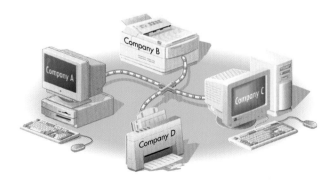

Most manufacturers follow industry standards so that their products will work with products developed by other companies.

International Standardization Organization

The International Standardization Organization (ISO) is an organization that develops product standards for the computer industry and coordinates the activities of other standards organizations.

The ISO's main objective is to allow networks to work together efficiently. The ISO developed the Open Systems Interconnection (OSI) model.

The OSI Model

The Open Systems Interconnection (OSI) model is a set of guidelines that describes all the aspects of the communication process. The OSI model also specifies how applications and devices should work in order to communicate with each other on a computer network.

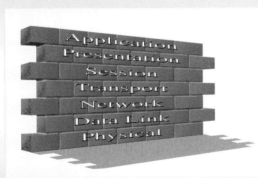

Layers

There are seven layers, or sections, in the OSI model. Each layer is responsible for one particular aspect of communication. For example, one layer may be used to specify how information is addressed to other computers. Another layer may be used to check errors during transfer.

Ensuring Compatibility

Before the OSI model was introduced, there was no standardized way to exchange information on a network. Many companies developed their own network devices without considering how they would work with or affect other devices on a network. When companies follow the OSI model, they ensure that their devices will communicate with other devices on a network.

OSI MODEL LAYERS

The OSI model has seven layers that describe the tasks that must be performed to transfer information on a network.

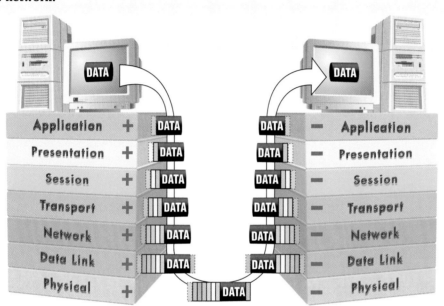

When data is being transferred over a network, it must pass through each layer of the OSI model. As the data passes through each layer, information is added to the data.

When the data reaches the destination, the data must again pass through the layers of the OSI model. The additional information is removed at each layer.

Application Layer

The Application layer is responsible for exchanging information between the programs running on a computer and other services on a network, such as a database or print service.

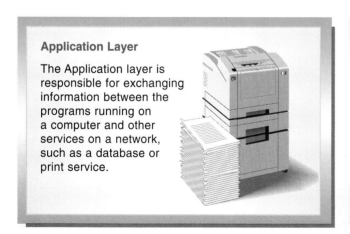

Presentation Layer

The Presentation layer formats information so that a software application can read the information.

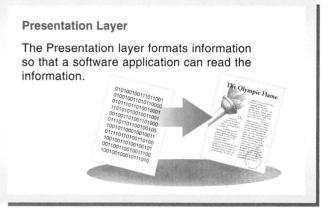

Session Layer

The Session layer determines how two devices communicate as well as establishes and monitors connections between computers.

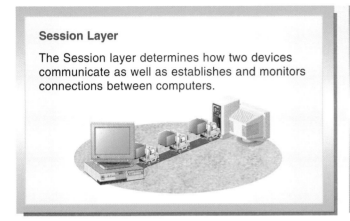

Transport Layer

The Transport layer corrects transmission errors and ensures that information is delivered reliably.

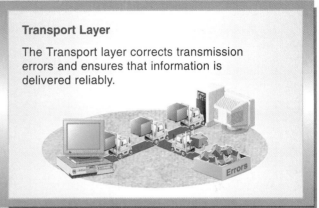

Network Layer

The Network layer identifies computers on a network and determines how to direct information transferring over a network.

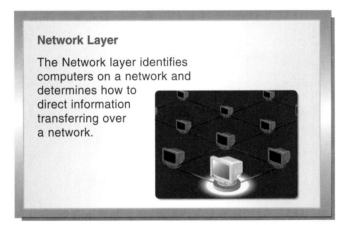

Data Link Layer

The Data Link layer groups data into sets to prepare the data for transferring over a network.

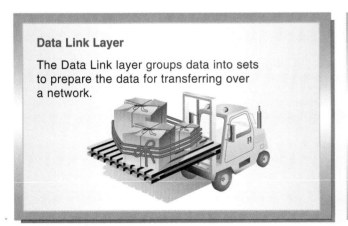

Physical Layer

The Physical layer defines how a transmission medium, such as a cable, connects to a computer. This layer also specifies how electrical information transfers on the transmission medium.

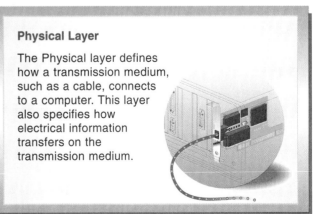

PROTOCOLS

Before two computers or network
devices can exchange information,
they must establish communication.
A network protocol allows two
devices to communicate using
the same set of rules.

Protocols

Protocols are the actual hardware or software
components that carry out the OSI model
guidelines for transferring information on a
network. A protocol may be one component
or a collection of components that carry out
a task.

Protocol Stacks

A protocol stack, or suite, is made up of multiple
protocols used to exchange information between
computers. One protocol in the stack might be
used to specify how network interface cards
communicate, while another might specify how
a computer reads information from the network
interface card.

Layers

A layer is a section of a protocol stack that is responsible for performing one particular aspect of information transfer. Since some protocols are capable of performing more than one function, one layer in a protocol stack may not necessarily correspond to one layer in the OSI model.

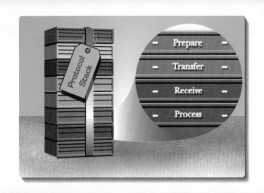

Compatibility

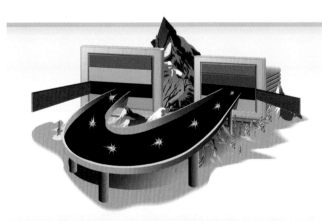

Computers on a network must use the same protocols to exchange information. A layer in a protocol stack on one computer must be able to communicate with the same layer in the protocol stack on another computer.

Standards

When a networking device is designed to communicate using an accepted protocol, the device can communicate with any other device that uses the same protocol. The OSI model and protocol standards help ensure networking devices will be able to work together on a network.

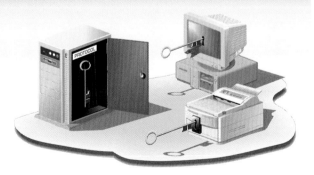

IPX/SPX PROTOCOLS

The IPX/SPX protocols combine to make the protocol suite that is used to transfer information on networks running the NetWare operating system.

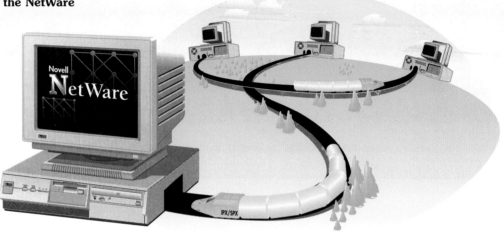

IPX

The Internetwork Packet Exchange (IPX) protocol is derived from a protocol developed by Xerox Corporation. The IPX protocol is used to transfer information between devices located on different networks and keep track of the locations of network devices in relation to other devices.

When the IPX protocol transfers data, the protocol does not monitor the transmission or check the reliability of the data.

SPX

The Sequenced Packet Exchange (SPX) protocol is an extension of the IPX protocol. The SPX protocol transfers information, but unlike IPX, SPX makes a connection between two network devices and monitors the transmission.

SPX also ensures the data exchanged has no errors.

Popular

Novell NetWare is the most popular network operating system used by large companies to connect computers.

Since many networks run NetWare, the IPX/SPX protocols are widely used and supported by many manufacturers.

Tunneling

Tunneling describes the process of using a protocol to transfer information through a different type of network. The IPX/SPX protocols support IP tunneling, so information can be transferred between NetWare networks using a TCP/IP network or the Internet.

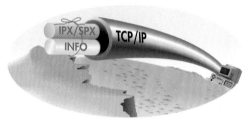

The information and IPX/SPX protocols are bundled within the TCP/IP protocol suite. When the information reaches its destination, the TCP/IP protocols are removed.

Ports

A port is a location in memory used by a program. Ports are virtual locations and exist only when the computer is running.

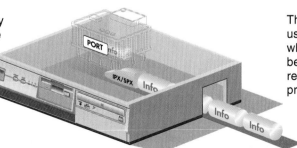

The IPX/SPX protocols use ports to indicate where information must be delivered in order to reach the appropriate program.

NETBEUI PROTOCOL

NetBEUI is a network protocol used in small Microsoft-based networks.

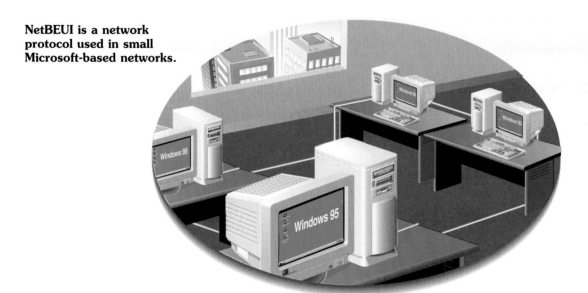

NetBIOS

NetBIOS (Network Basic Input/Output System) was developed by IBM as a way of allowing computers to communicate with each other on a network.

The NetBEUI (NetBIOS Extended User Interface) protocol was developed to improve upon NetBIOS and make it more efficient.

Performance

NetBEUI is a very small and efficient protocol that does not require a lot of computer resources, such as memory or processing power. NetBEUI can transfer information on a network much faster than many other protocols. However, NetBEUI is not used on wide area networks.

Microsoft

NetBEUI is found almost exclusively in networks that are based on products developed by Microsoft. All Microsoft products that connect to a network use the NetBEUI protocol.

Configuration

NetBEUI is quite simple to set up. When configuring a network computer using the NetBEUI protocol, the administrator must give the computer a unique name to identify it on the network. The administrator also needs to assign the computer to a workgroup, which will allow the computer to access a predetermined set of network resources.

Non-routable Protocol

The major disadvantage in using the NetBEUI protocol is that the protocol cannot be used on a large network. Many large networks use devices called routers to link parts of the network. Unfortunately, NetBEUI is a non-routable protocol, which means it cannot pass through network routers.

TCP/IP PROTOCOLS

TCP/IP is a collection, or stack, of protocols used to allow communication between networks with different types of computer systems. TCP/IP is the set of protocols used on the Internet.

Development

TCP/IP was originally developed in the late 1960s in response to the needs of the U.S. Department of Defense.

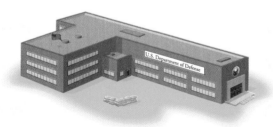

The TCP/IP protocol suite has been available for many years and has been repeatedly tested and improved. However, most TCP/IP protocols used to connect today's computers are the original protocols developed 30 years ago.

Popularity

TCP/IP quickly became a popular set of protocols because the companies that supplied products to the Department of Defense had to make their products support TCP/IP. As a result, many devices now support TCP/IP and many companies use TCP/IP to transfer information. The rapid growth of the Internet has also been a factor in the widespread popularity of TCP/IP.

Reroute

TCP/IP was designed to ensure that a collection of connected networks would be able to withstand a major disruption, such as war, that could damage several parts of the network. One of the main benefits of TCP/IP is that it can be used to easily reroute information around damaged parts of connected networks.

Network Types

TCP/IP is used on different types of networks including Ethernet, Token Ring and even networks using modem connections. Almost all networks are capable of supporting TCP/IP.

Open Standard

A major benefit of TCP/IP is that it is an open standard. This means that any company or person can design a device or software program that uses TCP/IP without having to pay a royalty or licensing fee.

There are many protocols that make up the TCP/IP protocol suite. Each protocol in the suite is responsible for performing a specific task.

TCP

Transmission Control Protocol (TCP) is used to transfer information between two devices on a TCP/IP network. TCP uses virtual ports to make connections and also monitors the transmission of information.

IP

Internet Protocol (IP) is responsible for addressing information and is used to direct information to its proper destination on a TCP/IP network.

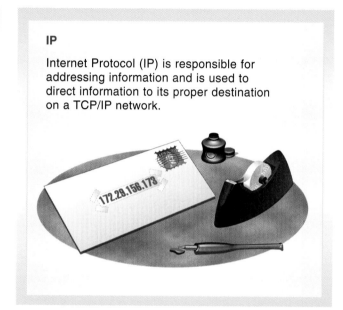

FTP

File Transfer Protocol (FTP) is one of the most widely recognized and used TCP/IP protocols. FTP is used to transfer documents between different types of computers on a TCP/IP network.

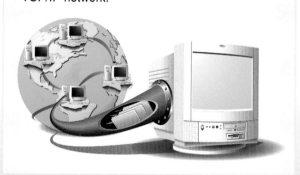

HTTP

HyperText Transfer Protocol (HTTP) is one of the most widely used protocols for transferring information on the Internet. HTTP is used to transfer information from Web servers to Web browsers.

UDP

User Datagram Protocol (UDP) uses virtual ports to transfer information between two applications on a TCP/IP network. UDP is slightly faster than the TCP protocol, but it is not as reliable.

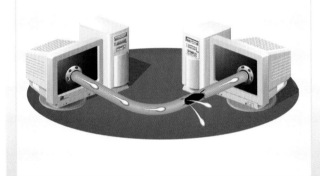

DHCP

Dynamic Host Configuration Protocol (DHCP) is used to allow communication between network devices and a server that administers IP numbers, called a DHCP server.

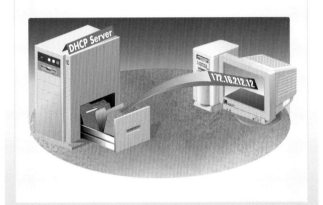

DNS

Domain Name System (DNS) is used to match Internet computer names to their corresponding IP numbers. DNS allows users to type a computer name, such as www.company.com, instead of an IP number, such as 192.168.53.3, to access a computer.

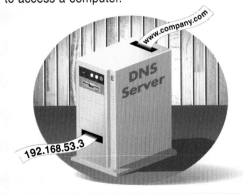

WINS

Windows Internet Name Service (WINS) is a protocol used on Microsoft-based TCP/IP networks. A server running WINS can match Microsoft network computer names to IP numbers. This allows computers on the Microsoft network to communicate with other networks and computers that use the TCP/IP suite.

CHAPTER 9

Protecting Network Data

It is important for every company to protect its network data. This chapter discusses the major threats to network data and how companies can protect their information.

THREATS TO NETWORK DATA

There are many ways that data can be lost, damaged or destroyed. Protecting important data is one of the primary responsibilities of a network administrator.

Computer Failure

One main cause of lost information is computer failure. Most storage devices, such as hard drives, are mechanical devices, which can become worn down and prone to failure. A storage device is often the first component to malfunction in a computer. When a storage device fails, all the data stored on the device may be lost.

Lack of Training

Network users who are not properly trained in how to access network data and use network equipment are likely to damage the data or equipment.

Users who have not been trained to recognize suspicious changes in their computer systems are also a threat to network data because they are unable to alert the system administrator to possible security breaches.

Accidents

The most frustrating way to lose data is by accident. A service technician performing maintenance or repairs on a computer may inadvertently erase the contents of a hard drive.

Computer users may also mistakenly erase information they think is unimportant, only to discover that the information was needed.

Fire

Faulty wiring can easily start a fire in a building. If a building catches fire, computers and the information stored on a network are often at risk of being destroyed.

Natural Disasters

Natural disasters can be devastating to a business. Disasters such as earthquakes and floods can often destroy all the information in a business in a matter of moments.

Most large organizations have disaster recovery programs that outline how these types of disasters are handled.

THREATS TO NETWORK DATA

Crackers

Crackers are people who enjoy the challenge of illegally breaking into computer systems. Crackers usually do not try to break into networks connected to the Internet.

If crackers do break into a network, they will probably not cause any damage, but they may be able to view information available on the network.

Electronic Eavesdropping

Sophisticated monitoring equipment can be used to record and decipher the electrical signals that are transmitted on network cables.

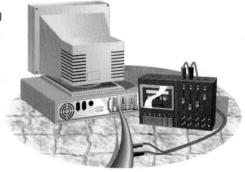

If a network is used to transfer confidential information, the network administrator should ensure that steps are taken to prevent electronic eavesdropping.

Theft

Almost every company is vulnerable to theft. Most computer systems are easily transported and can be very profitable for thieves.

Most computer thieves are very knowledgeable about computers and often strip the computers and sell the parts.

VIRUSES

A virus is a program that can cause a variety of problems, including the destruction of information on a computer system.

Infection

Files received on floppy disks and downloaded from FTP sites on the Internet are two ways networks can become infected with viruses.

No floppy disk or downloaded file should be used on a computer connected to a network until the disk or file has been scanned by an anti-virus program.

Detection

There are many anti-virus software programs available that will scan information stored on a computer to try and detect if there are any viruses on the computer.

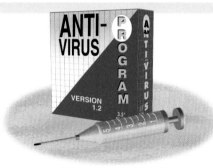

Many anti-virus programs can also remove viruses once they are detected. Some viruses cannot be removed without deleting information.

Backups

When a virus is discovered on a computer that is regularly backed up, it is important to determine when the computer became infected with the virus.

If a backup was performed while the virus existed on the computer, the computer may be reinfected if the backup copy is restored.

FIREWALLS

Firewalls protect network data by controlling the information that passes between a private network and the Internet.

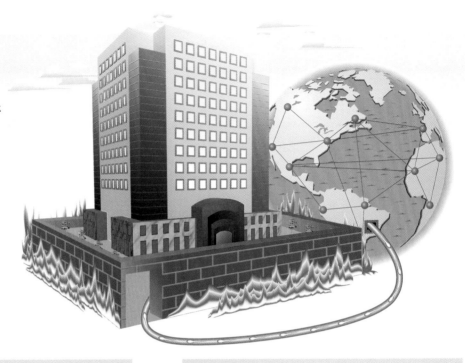

Firewalls

Most buildings are constructed with special walls designed to stop or slow the spread of fire through a building. A network firewall follows the same principle.

A network firewall is designed to prevent unauthorized individuals from accessing a private network.

Gateways

A gateway is usually a computer that acts as a connector between a private, internal network and another network, such as the Internet.

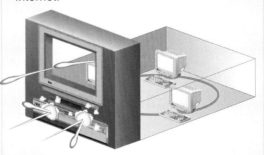

Gateways used as firewalls can transmit information from an internal network to the Internet. Gateways can also examine incoming information to determine if the information should be allowed entry to the network.

Filters

A firewall can be configured to filter information sent to a network. If the information does not originate from an approved source, then the information will be discarded. This is the simplest form of a firewall.

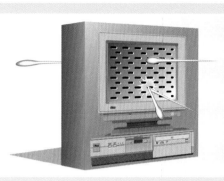

Sophisticated Filters

Some firewalls can actually examine each piece of information sent to or from a network. The firewall will then determine if the information should be allowed to pass through based on a customized set of rules defined by the system administrator.

Hardware and Software

Many companies use expensive, custom-built computers as firewalls. However, firewalls can also be software programs run on computers equipped with standard network interface cards.

Firewalls are usually designed for easy upgrading and reconfiguration to protect against new methods of attack.

PASSWORDS

Passwords protect network data against unauthorized access. When a network administrator configures a network to secure information and resources attached to the network, passwords are the first line of defense.

User name:

Password:

Users are normally assigned a password along with their user name. User names and passwords must always be kept secret to ensure network security.

Group Passwords

A group password allows members of a specific group to access certain network resources.

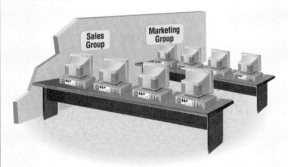

Sales Group

Marketing Group

Most operating systems allow network administrators to assign users to different groups at the same time. This allows the network administrator to be more flexible when assigning access to network resources.

Restrictions

Depending on the network operating system, a network administrator may be able to assign a password to individual resources connected to the network, such as a modem or a printer.

Password: blue@123

Password: jam#594

Before users can access a resource, they will be asked to enter the password. Assigning a password to resources can help regulate the use of certain resources, such as network fax machines.

FILE PERMISSIONS

File permissions can be used to control access to specific files, directories or storage devices attached to a network. File permissions are an important part of network security.

Common Permissions

Depending on the network operating system, a network administrator may be able to assign individual file permissions for each file, directory or storage device on the network. The most common file permissions include the following:

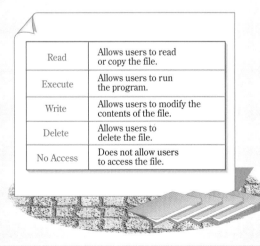

Read	Allows users to read or copy the file.
Execute	Allows users to run the program.
Write	Allows users to modify the contents of the file.
Delete	Allows users to delete the file.
No Access	Does not allow users to access the file.

File Activity Logs

One of the most useful features of a network is its ability to monitor file activity. Many network operating systems let network administrators examine who accessed files and when the files were accessed.

FILE ACTIVITY LOG

FILE NAME	ACCESSED BY	TIME
1997 Sales Report	James Garrett	9:35 AM
Technical Guidelines	Rose Henry	9:56 AM
June 1998 Budget	Marcie Bush	11:00 AM
Ongoing Projects	Hal Morrison	2:19 PM
Current Assignments	Alex Greene	3:08 PM
Marketing Proposal	Anna Stelleck	3:45 PM

By examining file activity, network administrators can adjust the file permissions to suit the requirements of the users.

BACK UP NETWORK DATA

Backing up data on a regular basis is an essential aspect of protecting information on a network. Backing up data creates an extra copy in case the original files are lost or damaged.

It is important to carefully schedule network backups to ensure that all important data is protected.

Backup Programs

A backup program helps the network administrator copy the files stored on a computer to a storage device, such as a tape cartridge.

Most storage devices come with a backup program specifically designed for use with the storage device.

Internet Backups

Many organizations now offer backup services using the Internet. If a company's network is connected to the Internet, it can easily transfer information to be backed up to an organization that will store the information.

Information can be restored by transferring the data back to the original company. Internet backup is most effective when backing up small amounts of information using a fast connection to the Internet.

Backup Strategies

When planning a backup strategy, a company must consider the amount of work it can afford to lose.

If the company cannot afford to lose the work accomplished in one day, a backup should be performed once a day. If the data does not change much during the week, a backup should be performed at least once a week.

Scheduled Backups

A company should create and then strictly follow a backup schedule. Most backup programs can be set to run automatically.

Many network administrators schedule backups for times when the network is not busy, such as lunchtime or the middle of the night.

Types of Backups

There are many ways that a network administrator can back up information. Most backup systems provide several types of backups.

For example, a full backup backs up all the files on a network computer. An incremental backup only backs up the files that have changed since the last backup. Daily backups only back up files that have been changed on that day.

TAPE BACKUP DEVICES

Tape drives are the most popular devices used for backing up data. Tape backup devices are used to copy the files stored on a computer onto a tape backup medium.

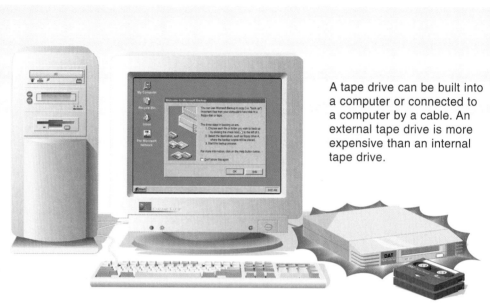

A tape drive can be built into a computer or connected to a computer by a cable. An external tape drive is more expensive than an internal tape drive.

Tape Backup Media

Tape backup media consists of plastic tape coated with magnetic particles, similar to the tape found in audio cassettes. Tape backup media can be stored on reels, but it is more commonly found in cartridges.

Care of Tape Backup Media

Tape backup cartridges should be stored in a cool, dry place, away from electrical equipment. If cartridges are stored for a long time, they should be rotated regularly to prevent the tape from stretching or sagging.

TYPES OF TAPE BACKUP DEVICES

Travan Drives

Travan drives are relatively inexpensive, but are not as fast as other types of tape backup devices. Travan cartridges can store up to 8 gigabytes (GB) of data and are used to back up information on individual computers or small networks.

DAT Drives

Digital Audio Tape (DAT) drives use technology originally developed for audio and video products. DAT drives are available in 8 millimeter (8 mm) and 4 mm versions. DAT cartridges can store up to 24 gigabytes (GB) of data. DAT drives are expensive, but the cartridges are inexpensive.

DLT Drives

Digital Liner Tape (DLT) drives are expensive, but can store large amounts of information on one cartridge. DLT cartridges can store up to 70 gigabytes (GB) of information and are used to back up information on large networks.

UNINTERRUPTIBLE POWER SUPPLIES

An Uninterruptible Power Supply (UPS) is used to provide power to a computer when the main electrical system fails.

Uninterruptible power supplies are often used on a network to ensure the network servers do not lose important data due to a power failure.

Power Backup

Most uninterruptible power supplies can detect a power failure and switch to battery power within a fraction of a second. Any computer connected to an uninterruptible power supply can continue to operate for a short period of time.

Safe Shutdown

An uninterruptible power supply enables users to finish their tasks and safely shut down their computers, but it is not intended to supply power for an extended period of time.

In the case of power loss, most uninterruptible power supplies will operate for at least 10 to 15 minutes.

Batteries

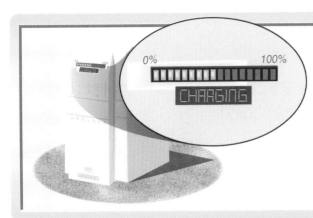

Most uninterruptible power supplies use rechargeable batteries to provide power to computers. As with all rechargeable batteries, special care must be taken to ensure optimal performance of an uninterruptible power supply. Some uninterruptible power supplies may require the user to fully discharge and recharge the batteries on a regular basis.

Surge Protection

A surge is a fluctuation in power. These surges, or spikes, can damage computer equipment. Many uninterruptible power supplies have built-in protection to prevent computers from being damaged by power surges.

Monitoring

Some uninterruptible power supplies also use sophisticated software to monitor and adjust the operation of the uninterruptible power supply.

When the power does fail, these software programs can safely shut down all the computers connected to the uninterruptible power supply.

FAULT TOLERANCE

Fault tolerance systems are designed to protect data by storing data on several devices in different locations. This helps ensure users will be able to access important information even if one storage device fails.

Server Protection

The servers on a network are often critical to the operation of a company. Companies cannot afford to have server failures nor can they afford to have their information destroyed. Fault tolerance is an effective method of protecting data on network servers.

RAID

The most common type of fault tolerance system found in large companies is called a Redundant Array of Inexpensive Drives (RAID) system. RAID systems often consist of several hard drives used to store duplicate data.

There are seven accepted levels of RAID, each specifying a different method for storing data. A higher RAID level does not indicate a higher level of protection.

FAULT TOLERANCE METHODS

Each RAID level uses one or more fault tolerance methods to prevent data loss.

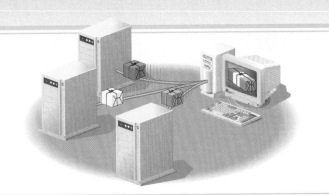

Striping

Striping involves breaking data into small pieces and distributing the data evenly over all the hard drives in the system. Striping is not the best method for protecting data because if one drive fails, all the data will be lost.

Mirroring

Mirroring occurs when all the data on a disk is duplicated onto another disk. For example, each time a user saves a change to a document, the change is saved in both locations.

Mirroring provides effective protection because if one drive fails, the mirrored drive can be used to store and access the same information.

Error Checking

Parity is the most common form of error checking. Data is always stored as a series of 1s and 0s. Parity ensures that errors have not occurred by verifying that the number of 1s in a series is consistently odd or even.

When parity information is stored in a RAID system, lost or damaged data can quickly be restored.

Certificate
A+
This is to certify that Alvin Lai
has successfully completed the A+ Certification
program sponsored by CompTIA.
Dated this 21st of February, 1998
GUIDELINES
• Use at least 8 characters for passwords.
• Do not leave work areas unattended.
• Keep passwords secret.
• Use only company disks.
• Log off nightly.
9:50 am
Testing ...
maranGraphics
PERFORMANCE 9000
Manual
Manual
Network Update
Time
Status
09:15 am
OK
09:30 am
OK
09:45 am
OK
10:00 am
10:15 am
10:30 am

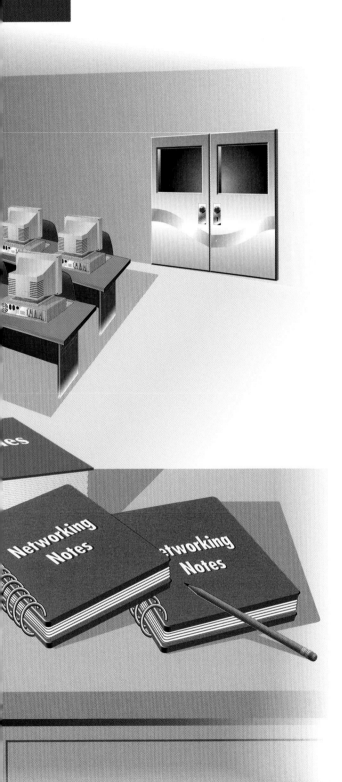

Network Administration

Proper administration is crucial to the success of any company network. This chapter examines network administration, performance, monitoring and much more.

NETWORK ADMINISTRATION

Administering a network can be a complex and demanding job. There are many responsibilities in ensuring a network runs efficiently, including the administration of individual user activities, network security and backups.

Responsibility

The main responsibility of the network administrator is to keep the network functioning at a level that suits the needs of all its users. Having the network function at all times is critical to a business. For this reason, the network administrator is often on call 24 hours a day.

Teams

A single network administrator is often not enough to manage a network effectively. Many companies have administration teams with different people responsible for different parts of the network. In some large corporations, there are entire departments dedicated to administering a network.

Training

It is important for network administrators to keep up-to-date with all current technologies. Network administrators should be constantly anticipating the future growth and maintenance of the networks they administer.

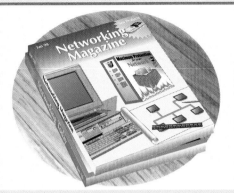

Network administrators also need to be aware of what new technologies they can use to overcome any future obstacles.

Records

Network administrators should keep very detailed records of all aspects of the network. Any changes made to the network, as well as the original plans for the network, should all be kept in a safe place.

Detailed records make it easier to plan the future growth of the network and are invaluable in helping troubleshoot any network problems.

Constraints

Network administrators must take into account many factors when performing their jobs. Monetary budgets and time constraints are the two most common factors that determine how network administrators perform their work.

NETWORK PERFORMANCE

The performance of a network determines how easily and efficiently the network can transfer information.

Fine-tuning Performance

Like most computer systems, a network is constantly fine-tuned to achieve optimal performance. A network that is constantly upgraded and optimized will be better suited to handle the requirements of its users before needs arise.

Performance Monitoring

All networks should be constantly monitored for indications of poor performance. Constant monitoring of network performance gives the administrator a good indication of how the network runs under normal circumstances. This makes it easier to detect problems when they first occur.

Monitoring and recording network performance can also help the administrator predict the future needs of the network.

Throughput

Throughput is the measurement of how fast data is transferred through different parts of the network.

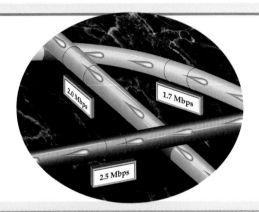

Throughput should be measured at various points in the network to help forecast where future transmission problems may occur.

Utilization Level

Each network is capable of transferring a specific amount of data. To determine the utilization level of the network, the administrator can compare the current amount of data being transferred to the maximum amount the network is capable of transferring.

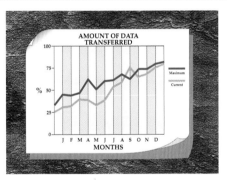

If the utilization level becomes too high, network performance may be seriously affected.

Errors

Every computer network has errors when transferring data. The more errors there are, the more network performance is affected. Software and hardware devices have been developed to detect many types of network errors, such as data loss.

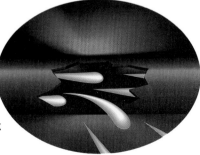

Errors must be carefully monitored so measures can be taken to avoid a serious decrease in network performance levels.

Network monitoring tools can be software or hardware that are used to monitor faults and activity on a network. The information collected by the monitoring tools is used to help manage and control the network.

Monitoring Network Devices

Network monitoring tools are used to communicate with devices that are connected to a network.

Each network device, such as a hub, router or network printer, can communicate with the network monitoring tool and inform the tool of the device's current status.

Compatibility

Network devices and monitoring tools must be compatible and must use the same method of communication before they can exchange information.

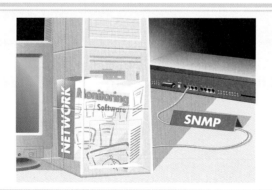

Simple Network Management Protocol (SNMP) is the most common method of communication used by network devices and monitoring tools.

Network Monitoring Hardware

Some network monitoring tools are special hardware devices that are physically connected to the network.

Hardware network monitoring tools can be hand-held devices or customized laptop computers.

Network Monitoring Software

Some network monitoring tools can be software that runs on a computer attached to the network.

Network monitoring software uses the processing power of a computer to collect and analyze information gathered from the network.

Constant Updates

Devices on a network can be configured to send status information to the network monitoring tools at regular intervals.

Constant updates on the status of all the devices on a network can give the network administrator an overview of how the network is currently operating. The administrator can configure devices to report their status at intervals of minutes or hours.

NETWORK MANAGEMENT SOFTWARE

Network management software helps network administrators control and configure computer networks. Network management software can help save time and money.

Administration

Network administrators use network management software to control all parts of a network. The software can be used to activate or shut down network devices, such as hubs or servers.

Management software may also be used to control user access to a network. For example, the software could be used to restrict parts of a network to authorized users.

Performance

Network management software can be used to help increase the performance of a network. Most network management software can direct network traffic around slower sections of the network.

The software can also be used to direct traffic around malfunctioning components, such as routers, which may lead to information loss.

Remote Access

Most network management software allows network administrators to connect to the software from a remote location. This allows the network to be controlled by administrators who work in multiple locations.

Remote access is also useful for companies that have many offices scattered across a city, but have only one network administrator.

Alerts

Network management software can be used to alert a system administrator or team of administrators when part of the network requires attention, such as a failing hard drive on a network computer.

Alerts can be sent in many forms, including e-mail or pager messages.

Expansion

Network management software is often used to indicate when a network should be expanded.

For example, network management software has many reporting features that can indicate when a network is becoming too busy and can no longer efficiently handle the amount of activity on the network.

NETWORK POLICIES

All network administrators should have a set of policies determining how users access and use the network. When network policies are followed, many network problems can be avoided.

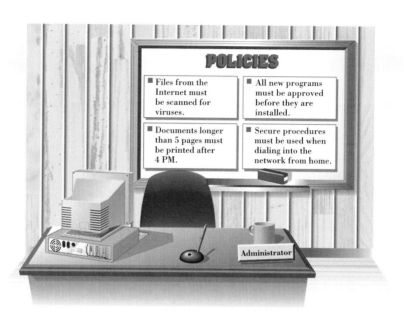

Network Guidelines

Each network policy should contain detailed guidelines describing how users interact with the network. For example, guidelines may be used to determine what actions users should take if they encounter a virus.

The network administrator is usually responsible for developing and implementing network guidelines.

Security Guidelines

Network policies should always include guidelines regarding the use of passwords and other security procedures. When users do not follow security guidelines, network security may be compromised.

To ensure network security, the network administrator should constantly work with users and company management to create and enforce the guidelines.

Training

Many policies concerning computer networks include technical procedures, such as properly shutting down a malfunctioning computer. The network administrator should ensure that users are trained to perform any procedures that may be required of them.

Updating Policies

Networks can change considerably as they grow. Small peer-to-peer networks can change into large client/server networks in a matter of months. As the network grows, it is important to update policies and guidelines to accommodate the new system.

Policy Enforcement

Network guidelines contain instructions that may be vital to the continued and optimal operation of a network. If these guidelines are not followed, a network disaster may occur. It is important for companies to implement appropriate disciplinary procedures for users who do not follow network policies.

NETWORK CONSULTANTS

An independent network consultant or a consulting firm is often contracted when a company is planning a major network upgrade or the installation of a new network.

Computer Stores

Companies with small networks can usually install and upgrade their networks with minimal assistance. Many computer stores provide network planning and installation services as well as troubleshooting advice for customers who purchase their network hardware and software components at the store.

Hiring a Consultant

Only the largest companies have the necessary staff and resources to competently complete work on large computer networks. Whenever a company is planning to perform a major upgrade or install a new computer network, the company should always consider retaining the services of a consultant or consulting firm for assistance.

Projects

The network administrator should verify whether potential consultants have worked on projects similar to the one for which they are applying.

While some consultants may be experts with one particular network operating system, they may have no experience with the operating system required for the current project.

Project Time Frame

The consultant often completes the planning of a network upgrade or installation. A network administrator should ensure that the consultant is aware of any resource or time constraints that may affect the outcome of the project. This can help ensure that the project will be completed within the time frame required by the company.

Contracts

A company should always have a written contract with any consultants that are hired. Most consultants also have their own service contracts.

Situations often arise where it is difficult to determine who is responsible for correcting a problem. A written contract will help resolve these types of issues.

Availability

Fixing problems in a new or upgraded network often entails disrupting the use of the network and should be done when the network is not in use, such as evenings or weekends.

The administrator should make sure that the consultant would be available at these times.

Support

The network administrator should make sure that any consultant that is hired has the necessary resources to offer support.

Depending on the type of project, the network administrator may need 24-hour access to assistance or spare parts.

Compatibility

When a network administrator hires a consultant, the consultant will often be working with the company for an extended period of time.

The consultant should be compatible with the network administrator, any staff that the consultant has to work with and the company itself.

QUALIFICATIONS

References

One of the most important steps in hiring a consultant is checking references.

A competent consultant will always be able to supply a list of previous customers that the network administrator may contact in order to help evaluate the skill level of the consultant.

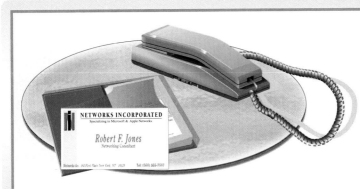

Referrals

Network administrators may want to ask other people they trust in the industry which consultant or consulting firm they use. Referrals are often the best way of finding a good networking consultant.

Certifications

There are many certifications available for a wide range of software and hardware used in computer networks.

If possible, a network administrator should hire a consultant who is certified to install and service the network resources the company wants to use.

Network Certifications

Many hardware and software manufacturers provide certifications for people in computing professions. This chapter discusses the various types of hardware and software product certifications available.

INTRODUCTION TO CERTIFICATIONS

Certifications confirm levels of knowledge and expertise that are recognized throughout the computer industry. Many hardware and software manufacturers provide various types of product certifications.

Classroom Instruction

Most certification programs are taught in a classroom environment. Classroom instruction has many benefits, including easy access to an instructor if a student has questions.

The main drawbacks of classroom-based training are that the classes are very time-consuming and are often conducted during business hours.

Computer-based Training

Computer-based training is becoming more widely used as a means of enabling people to receive technical certification. In computer-based training, a software program guides the student through the training material.

Some programs even adjust the content according to the student's level of knowledge. Computer-based training allows people to work at their own pace on their own computers.

Modules

Most certification programs are made up of modules, or sections. People can choose different modules depending on the area they wish to learn about. For example, a communications engineer may choose modules focusing on data transfer. A technical support person may concentrate more on modules concerning software or hardware repair.

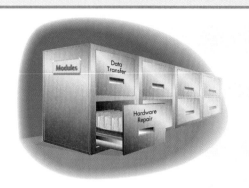

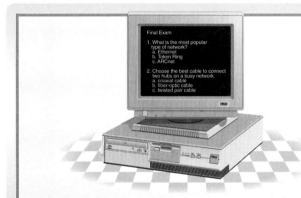

Testing

Testing is usually done in a registered training center. Most tests are performed on a computer and consist of multiple-choice questions. The students usually find out whether they have passed shortly after they have completed the exam.

Experience

While a certificate is a valuable asset, it is equally important to have hands-on experience. A system administrator who is certified and has hands-on experience is considered the most qualified professional in the field.

MICROSOFT CERTIFICATION

Microsoft offers a wide range of hardware and software certifications.

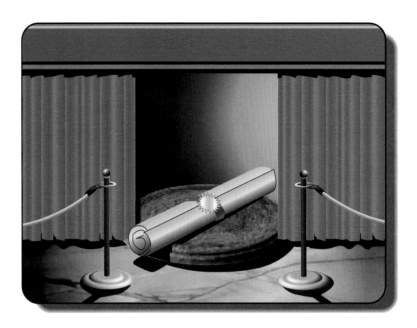

Certifications

There are currently four Microsoft certifications available. Certifications include Microsoft Certified Professional (MCP), Microsoft Certified Systems Engineer (MCSE), Microsoft Certified Trainer (MCT), and Microsoft Certified Solution Developer (MCSD).

Since there are a variety of certifications available, companies should ensure that their administrators or network consultants have the appropriate Microsoft certifications.

Recognition

Microsoft certifications are some of the most widely recognized certifications in the computing industry. The MCSE designation is recognized worldwide.

Service professionals who work with Microsoft products should have Microsoft certification.

Training

There are many ways to train for Microsoft certifications. Many schools offer classes over the Internet and in classrooms. There are also many books available that will assist people in preparing for Microsoft certification exams on their own.

Exams

Each certification is acquired by passing a number of exams specified by Microsoft. The exams must be written at a Microsoft-approved testing center, where the exams may be supervised. Microsoft has many testing and training centers throughout the world.

Up-to-date Certifications

Microsoft is constantly updating the courses required to achieve certification.

As new Microsoft products become available and older products become obsolete, Microsoft adds and removes courses to ensure that people are certified to support the most current products.

NOVELL CERTIFICATION

Novell manufactures NetWare, one of the most successful network operating systems. Novell also provides certifications for people who want to use and maintain the NetWare operating system.

Variable Skill Levels

Novell offers certification programs for people of all skill levels, from the user who wants to administer a small network with only a few computers to the support professional who wishes to administer a wide area network with thousands of users.

Designations

Novell offers certifications for many different professions. Novell's current certifications include Certified Novell Salesperson (CNS), Certified Novell Administrator (CNA), Certified Novell Engineer (CNE), Master CNE, Certified Internet Professional (CIP) and Certified Novell Instructor (CNI).

Training

Training is available in a variety of formats. Novell was one of the first network operating system manufacturers to offer comprehensive training. Classroom-based training is available at many locations.

For people who prefer to learn at their own pace, training books and CD-ROMs are also available.

Novell Press

Novell publishes its own line of books that contain information about its courses and products. Many Novell books allow people to study at home before a certification exam.

Networks

Since networking products form the core of the Novell product line, Novell's certification training focuses on these types of products.

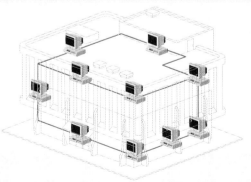

As a result, people with Novell certification tend to be competent not only with Novell's own NetWare products, but in other areas of networking as well.

SUN JAVA CERTIFICATION

Java is a programming language created by Sun Microsystems that can be used on computer networks. Sun Java certification provides programmers and developers with the necessary skills to create programs with Java.

Java

Java is a relatively new programming language developed to provide an easier way to write programs that can run on different computers and operating systems. Many hardware and software manufacturers now endorse the use of Java to create new software applications.

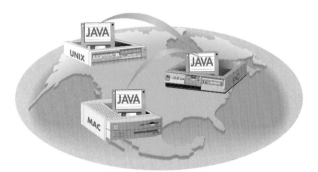

The Java programming language is also very popular for creating small programs, called applets, that can be used on the World Wide Web or intranets.

Java Restrictions

Although Sun Microsystems created the Java programming language, they do not place any restrictions on the use of the language.

Copyright issues are not a concern when creating and distributing programs written in Java.

Designations

Java offers two certification designations. The Sun Certified Java Programmer designation is for people who plan to create Java programs. The Sun Certified Java Developer designation is for people who want to create more complex applications that use the Java language.

Certification Versions

The development tools used to create Java programs are constantly being updated and revised. Sun Java certifications are only valid for a single version of the Java development tools. If a person wishes to work with a newer version of the development tools, the certification should be updated.

Exams

Exams for Java certification take about two hours and must be completed in an approved testing facility.

As with most other certification programs, the exams are comprised of multiple-choice and short-answer questions.

Sun Microsystems offers certification programs for people who want to administer systems or networks running the Solaris operating system.

Solaris

Solaris is an operating system used on high-performance computers.

Solaris is a UNIX-based operating system that is found in many companies and organizations whose networks are connected to the Internet.

Certified Solaris Administrator

The Certified Solaris Administrator (CSA) designation indicates that a person has successfully taken the test to administer a network running the Solaris operating system.

The Certified Solaris Administrator designation is recognized worldwide. Many people acquire the CSA designation as a step toward improving their career opportunities.

Up-to-date Certifications

Both the Solaris operating system and the computers that run the Solaris operating system are constantly changing.

The training program for the Certified Solaris Administrator designation is frequently modified to reflect new technologies and changes in the operating system.

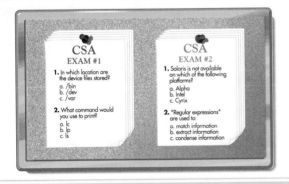

Exams

The Certified Solaris Administrator designation is earned by passing two exams. The exams consist of approximately 100 multiple-choice questions. It takes approximately 90 minutes to complete each of the exams. The exams can be taken together or separately.

Compatibility

Because Solaris is a UNIX-based operating system, the skills learned by Certified Solaris Administrators can be applied to other UNIX operating systems.

People who have a Solaris certification are usually capable of administering other UNIX operating systems.

A+ CERTIFICATION

A+ certification is used to standardize the level of knowledge that computer service and support personnel have. A+ is a nationally recognized, industry-wide standard of computer knowledge.

CompTIA

Computing Technology Industry Association (CompTIA) is an association of some of the most renowned computer hardware and software manufacturers in the world. CompTIA sponsors the A+ certification program.

Computer Service Professionals

The A+ certification is recognized by people who perform a wide range of services in the computer service profession. Help desk personnel, service technicians and computer resellers often find it beneficial to have A+ certification.

The A+ certification was first launched in 1993, but many service professionals have not yet acquired the A+ certification.

Modules

In order to receive the A+ certification, a person must pass two exams. The first exam, called the core module, tests general computing and customer service knowledge.

The second exam, or module, allows the person to specialize in the Windows and DOS or Macintosh operating systems.

Networks

While the A+ certification does not ensure that a person can service or maintain a computer network, the certification does indicate that the person has a basic overall knowledge of the computers found on most networks.

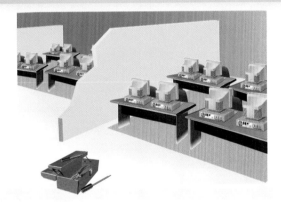

Advantages

People who have the A+ certification are generally recognized as being able to service, maintain, install and upgrade personal computers and other related devices.

Since A+ is such a widely recognized standard, this certification provides a level of credibility and gives a competitive edge to people who become certified.

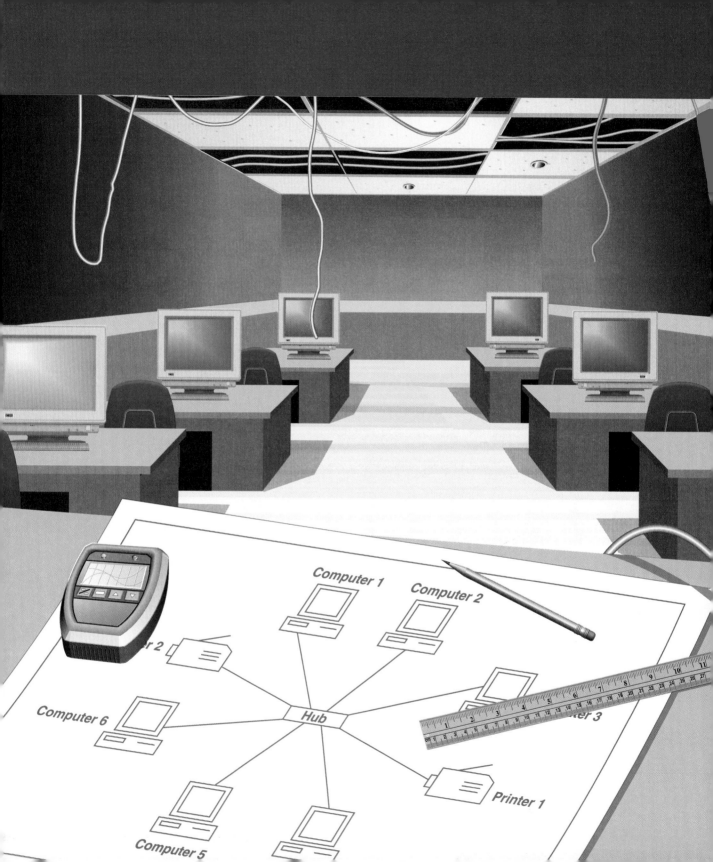

CHAPTER 12

Installing or Upgrading a Network

Several factors should be considered when planning the installation or upgrade of a network. This chapter explains how to evaluate the current network, choose the proper network hardware and much more.

PLANNING A NETWORK

Planning is the most important aspect of installing a new computer network. When planning a new network, there are many factors to consider.

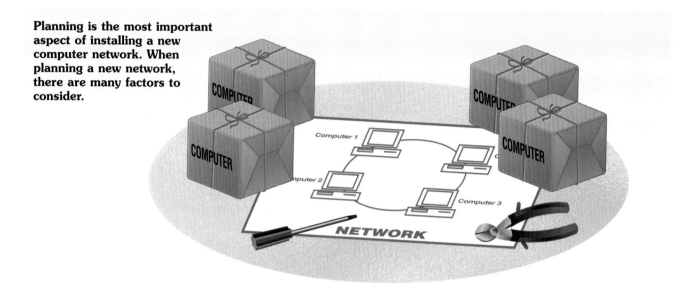

Network Sizes

Current and future network sizes are two of the most important aspects to consider when planning a new network. Some network operating systems and architectures are optimized for certain network sizes.

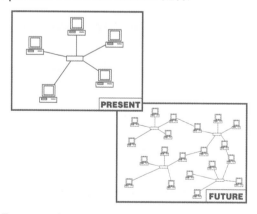

For example, a peer-to-peer network is adequate for a small network of 10 users, but would be unsuitable for a network of a thousand users.

Bandwidth

The amount of information the network will be required to transfer at once helps determine the type of network a company needs.

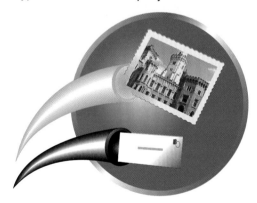

For example, a graphics company may use a fiber-optic cable based network to transfer large image files. A network used primarily for exchanging e-mail could use a wire-cable based network.

Network Location

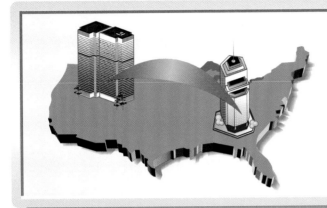

The location of the network must be considered before examining any other aspects of the network, such as the network operating system and necessary protocols. For example, a single network in an office building will have different protocol and security requirements than two branch offices connected by the Internet.

Logs

Network administrators should keep track of any decisions made or procedures performed while planning a network. Problems encountered while planning the network, as well as any steps taken to resolve the problems, should also be recorded.

If another person has to work on the network or if the network planning process needs to be re-evaluated, accurate records can be useful.

Professional Help

While simple networks can often be put together by someone with an intermediate knowledge of computers, any network larger than a few users should be planned by computer professionals. There are many firms that can help with the planning and installation of a new network.

UPGRADING A NETWORK

There are many reasons why
a network administrator may
need to upgrade a network.

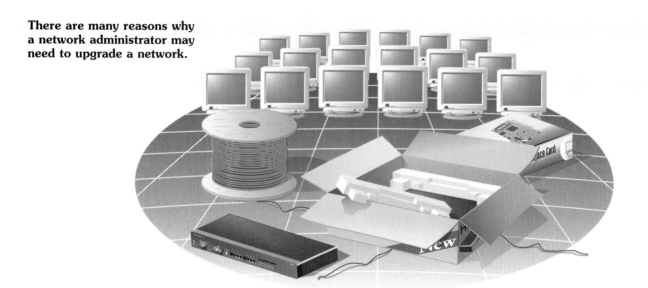

Company Growth

Many networks were originally designed to
be used by only a small number of people.
However, as businesses grow, networks need
to be upgraded and enhanced to accommodate
the increase in the number of employees who
need access to the networks.

Obsolete Equipment

Many networks may use networking devices that
are old and obsolete. Some older network devices
may no longer be available to purchase. When
older network devices fail, replacement hardware
can be hard to find. Older networking equipment
can also limit the expansion possibilities for
a network.

Protection

For many companies, a network is crucial for business. If the network is unavailable, a company's capabilities may be seriously affected. Networks are often upgraded to provide protection in case part of the network fails. Upgrading can help improve data backups and other security procedures.

Administration

Administering older networks can be very time-consuming. Many newer networks and network devices can be administered using software applications from a central computer. In some cases, upgrading a network and the network devices can reduce the time and effort required for administering the network.

Software Upgrades

Many software applications, such as database programs, may be upgraded to run on networks. A network administrator may need to upgrade a network so it is capable of operating efficiently with the new software applications.

EVALUATE CURRENT NETWORK

A network administrator should examine the status of the network before an upgrade to determine what parts of the network will be affected by the upgrade.

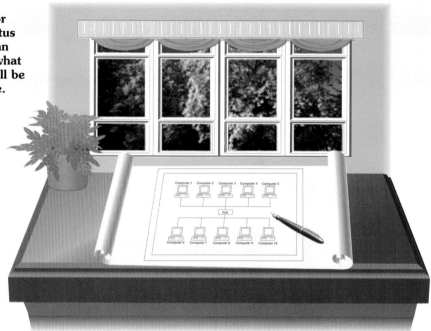

Logs

Every network should have a log to record any changes made to the network. The network administrator should be able to use the log to determine what types of hardware and software are currently used on the network. Reviewing the log can help the administrator determine which areas of the network need to be upgraded.

Inventory

The network administrator should take a complete inventory of all the components of the network. When choosing new hardware or software, the network administrator will need a complete list of all current network devices to ensure the new devices will be compatible with the existing network.

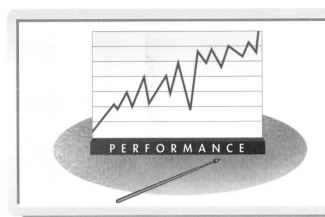

Performance

The network should be evaluated to determine how different parts affect the overall performance of the network. Many monitoring tools are available that can pinpoint the cause of problems, such as information bottlenecks on a network.

Technical Support

The network administrator should evaluate the technical support requirements of the current network, as well as how the upgraded network will be supported.

A new or upgraded network often requires staff training or obtaining the services of a company that can service and support the network.

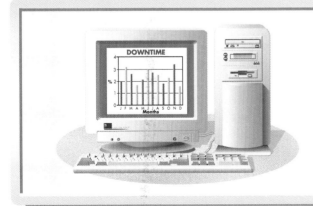

Downtime

Every network has periods, called downtime, when the network does not function due to failure or other factors. The goal of every administrator is to have no downtime when the network is needed. A network administrator should evaluate current downtime levels and try to determine how downtime can be eliminated.

DETERMINE NETWORK DESIGN

Whether building a new network or upgrading an existing one, predetermining the design of the network will give administrators an outline of the overall network.

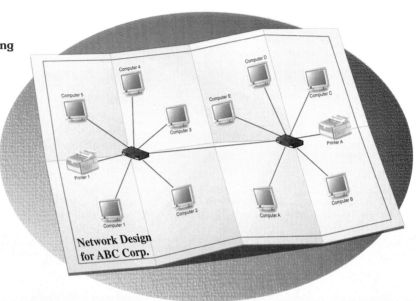

Network Design for ABC Corp.

Network Structure

The star structure is the simplest and most widely used network structure. Unless there are specific reasons for using another structure, such as a ring or bus, network administrators should always use the star structure since it is easy to administer and expand.

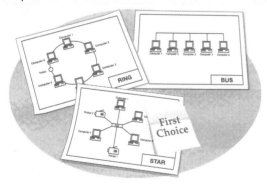

Network Operating System

Each network operating system has its own set of strengths and weaknesses. Many small networks use a peer-to-peer network operating system, such as Windows 95.

If a network has more than twenty users, the network administrator should consider using a client/server network operating system such as Windows NT or Novell NetWare.

Network Architecture

There are many network architectures available, but in most cases the Ethernet architecture is preferred. Ethernet is popular and easy to implement. However, upgrading to Ethernet may not be a feasible alternative if the current network needs to be compatible with other network architectures, such as Token Ring or ARCnet.

Files and Applications

Some network designs and architectures are better suited for transferring specific types of information. For example, if many network users save large files created in drawing programs, the network may slow down. Network administrators must make sure the network is capable of efficiently working with all files and applications.

Future Needs

A network should be designed with the future needs of the network in mind. No matter how large a network is, a network administrator will almost certainly have to expand or modify it in the future. Considering future expansion when designing a network will make network modifications easier.

There are many types of architectures that may be considered for new or upgraded networks.

Ethernet

Most new networks should use one of the Ethernet standards available. Ethernet is the most popular and best supported of all architectures and should be compatible with any future developments.

A company that invests in Ethernet technology today should be able to easily upgrade its network in the future.

Fast/Gigabit Ethernet

Fast/Gigabit Ethernet transfers information at speeds of up to 100 megabits per second (Mbps) and is generally referred to as 100BaseT. There are several types of 100BaseT available.

100BaseTX is Fast/Gigabit Ethernet that uses Category 5 unshielded twisted pair cable to transfer information. 100BaseT4 is another type of Fast/Gigabit Ethernet that uses four pairs of Category 3 unshielded twisted pair cables to transfer information.

100BaseFX

100BaseFX is similar to Fast/Gigabit Ethernet, but it uses fiber-optic cable to transfer information, as opposed to unshielded twisted pair cable. The glass or clear plastic core in the fiber-optic cable used on a 100BaseFX network is thicker than in other types of fiber-optic cables, which makes it easier to work with.

100VG-AnyLAN

100VG-AnyLAN is a version of Ethernet that transmits information at speeds of up to 100 megabits per second (Mbps). 100VG-AnyLAN can be configured to give priority to certain types of information, such as audio and video. 100VG-AnyLAN is often found on networks that use videoconferencing.

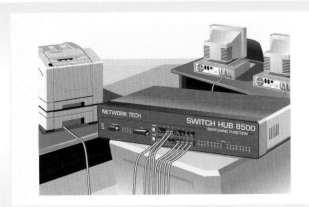

Switched Ethernet

On a regular Ethernet network, all the devices must share the available bandwidth. On a switched Ethernet network, each device can use the full bandwidth to communicate. A conventional Ethernet network can be transformed into a switched Ethernet network by replacing existing hubs with switching hubs.

UPGRADING TRANSMISSION MEDIA

When upgrading a network, the transmission media is one of the most important aspects to consider. If a greater speed is required or a new network architecture is being used, the transmission media may have to be replaced.

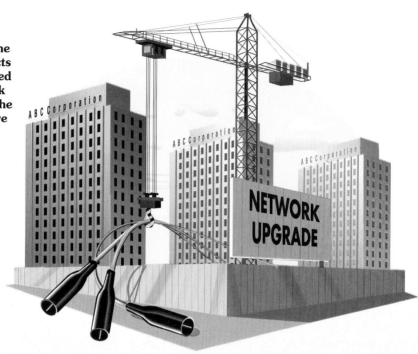

Speed

Many existing network cables may not have the ability to transfer information fast enough for today's applications. Most new networks are capable of transferring information at speeds of up to 100 megabits per second (Mbps), while older networks may only be able to transfer information at a fraction of that speed.

Cost

Many inexpensive network devices are available that allow easy connection to a network using shielded or unshielded twisted pair cable. Networks that use older cable types, such as coaxial cable, may not be able to take advantage of current, inexpensive network hardware.

Coaxial Cable

In the past, most networks used coaxial cable to transfer information. Coaxial cable has many limitations that may hinder the future expansion of a network.

Fiber-optic Cable

Fiber-optic cable is a very fast, but expensive, transmission medium. Fiber-optic cable is often used to link busy devices together, such as hubs and routers.

Twisted Pair Cable

Shielded and unshielded twisted pair cables are the most common types of cables used in new networks. When upgrading an existing network or installing a new network, the network administrator should consider using good quality twisted pair cable.

**Shielded
Twisted Pair**

**Unshielded
Twisted Pair**

Unshielded Twisted Pair Cable Ratings

Unshielded twisted pair cable is rated by the minimum speed at which information can be transferred using the cable. Most new cable that is installed is Category 5 unshielded twisted pair cable, which is adequate for most current and future networks.

CATEGORY	RATING
Category 1	not rated
Category 2	1 Mbps
Category 3	16 Mbps
Category 4	20 Mbps
Category 5	100 Mbps

INSTALLING CABLE

Network cable is used to connect all devices on a computer network. It is essential that network cable is installed correctly.

Professional Installation

There are many factors that must be considered to ensure that network cable is installed correctly. If the network administrator is installing more than a few computers on a network, a professional cable installer should be hired to install the cable.

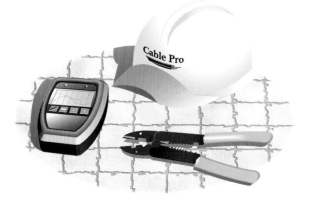

Professional cable installers have sophisticated testing equipment to ensure that cables function correctly.

Interference

Many electrical devices in modern offices can cause interference on network cable. Photocopiers, fluorescent lighting and electric motors are all common causes of interference.

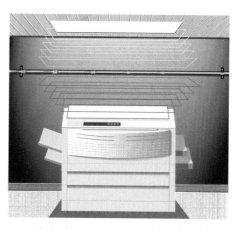

To prevent interference, a network administrator should install network cable at least two feet from any source of electrical signals.

Conduits

When installing new cable, the network administrator should consider the use of special cable conduits.

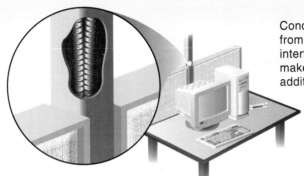

Conduits can protect cable from any outside electrical interference. Conduits also make it easier to install additional cable in the future.

Jacks

Most cable is accessed by jacks that are installed in the walls of a building. Before a jack is installed, the network administrator should determine where the office furniture will be located.

Since a length of cable will have to connect the computer to the jack, jacks should be placed in convenient locations.

Fire Hazards

Cable is often installed in the space above a dropped ceiling, which is used to distribute air throughout a building.

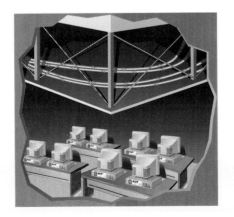

Some types of cables are constructed of material, which if exposed to fire, emits poisonous fumes that can spread quickly throughout a building. To avoid this type of hazard, many local authorities require special cable to be used.

CHOOSING NETWORK HARDWARE

Network hardware are the physical devices used on a network. It is important to choose the correct hardware when installing or upgrading a network.

Purchasing Hardware

There are many locations where computer hardware can be purchased. If good technical support is required, products should be purchased from a company that specializes in computer networks. Network products can also be purchased from local computer stores, as well as by mail order.

Professional Consultants

Many network consulting firms will evaluate network design plans to make recommendations and determine if anything has been missed. Network consulting firms often sell the necessary computer hardware.

When installing a network for more than 10 users, the network administrator may want to consider having professionals design and install the entire network.

Cost

Most buying decisions are limited by the amount of money a company budgets for network hardware. Network administrators should consider that price is often an indicator of product quality. Expensive network devices often perform better and are more manageable than inexpensive devices.

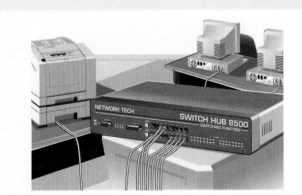

Types of Hardware

Since many devices can perform multiple functions, the choice between different types of network hardware can be difficult. Hubs that perform switching functions should be used where possible when connecting devices and networks together. With the exception of some complex tasks on very large networks, switching hubs are the best choice for most tasks.

Network Interface Cards

Network interface cards are the most common hardware devices on a network. The type of network architecture used is a factor that determines which network interface card is required. A network interface card must also be compatible with the computer in which it is installed.

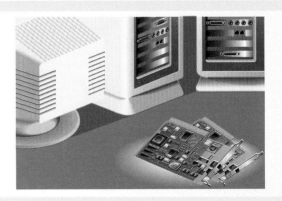

INSTALLING NETWORK HARDWARE

There are several factors to consider when installing network hardware. It is important to ensure that network hardware is functional and protected when installed, so it will continue to work properly.

Hardware Testing

Most network hardware components include a self-testing system. The network administrator should check new network hardware immediately after it has been delivered to ensure that it is functioning properly.

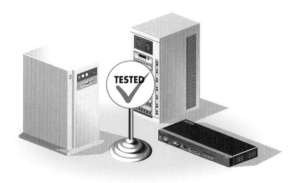

The installation or upgrade of a network could be delayed if faulty or incorrect hardware is installed before adequate testing.

Security

Network hardware is usually very expensive and is important to the operation of the entire network. Any damage to network hardware may affect network access for many users.

To prevent damage, network hardware should be kept in a secure location that can be locked and that is not accessible to unauthorized people.

Computer Rooms

It is easier for an administrator to maintain a network when all of the important components are located in one area. Many companies now have computer rooms that are strictly used to house much of the computer equipment on the network. This gives the administrator easy access to the network hardware.

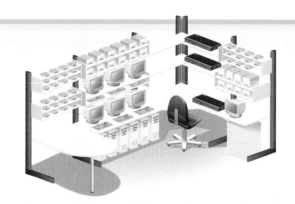

Organizational Racks

Many companies have racks that are used to organize network hardware components, such as hubs and servers.

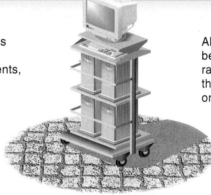

Almost all network hardware can be placed on an organizational rack. This allows easy access to the devices while keeping them organized and tidy.

Client Computers

Client computers are usually the easiest part of the network hardware installation, since they only require a network interface card to connect to the network.

Network interface cards usually take a few minutes to install. Many computers now have built-in network interface cards.

INSTALLING THE NETWORK OPERATING SYSTEM

A network operating system controls all the activity on a network. To ensure the network will run smoothly, several factors should be considered during and after the installation of the network operating system.

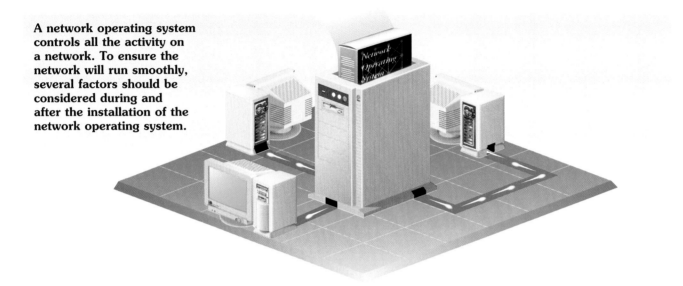

Complex Installation

Installing a network operating system is often the most complex part of upgrading an existing network or installing a new network. Many network operating systems require at least two or three hours to perform a basic installation.

Unless the network operating system is a basic system, qualified professionals should perform the installation.

Connecting Devices

Network administrators should have all the network devices connected and functional before starting to install the network operating system.

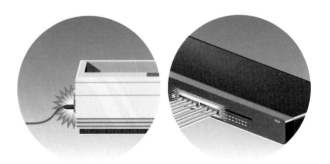

The operating system may need to communicate with network devices, such as printers or hubs, during the installation.

Transferring Information

Once the network operating system has been set up on a client/server network, information will need to be transferred to the file servers.

Network administrators should carefully plan what information will be stored and where on the servers the information will be stored.

Security

After installing the network operating system, all the security settings should be thoroughly reviewed. One approach to security is to restrict access to all resources and information. The network administrator can grant users access to certain parts of the network as needs arise.

Managing Users

Once the network is functioning, the network administrator will often have to set up user accounts and assign passwords. The administrator can set up workgroups for users who need access to the same set of resources. If many users need to be set up, the network operating system may allow the network administrator to automate the task.

CONFIGURING CLIENT COMPUTERS

Each user on a network usually has a client computer. A client computer must be configured before it can be used on the network.

Configuration

The amount of configuration required by a client computer depends on the type of network. Configuring the client may be as simple as assigning a name to the client or as complex as altering the software and hardware settings on the computer.

Network Drivers

A network interface card is the only hardware that is required to connect a client computer to the network. A special software program, called a driver, is usually required before the network interface card can communicate with other devices on the network.

Most network interface cards come with multiple drivers that enable the cards to communicate with many different types of networks.

Applications

On a network, an application such as a word processor only needs to be installed on a server. The clients on the network can then access the application. However, the network administrator must configure each client computer to save each user's settings for the application, such as fonts and color schemes.

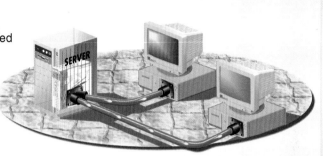

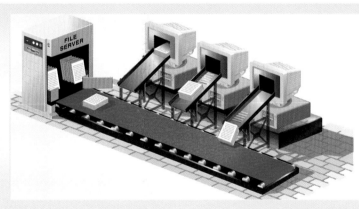

Information

Instead of saving information on its own hard drive, a client computer can save information on a file server on the network. Most client computers on a network will need to be configured so they can access the file server.

Resources

Other computers attached to the network may use resources, such as printers and modems, attached to a client computer. Before other computers can access a resource, the client must be configured to use and share the resource. The client computer must also be turned on and logged on to the network before the resource can be used.

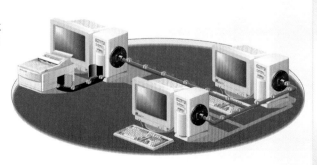

TESTING THE NETWORK

Once the entire network is installed and configured, the network should be tested to ensure that all the devices are functioning and information is transferring properly.

Notes

The types of problems encountered on one network will be different from problems on another network. When trying to resolve a problem, a network administrator should always keep detailed notes for future reference.

Accurate notes will make it easier to repair recurring network problems. Many problems may seem to resolve themselves, only to reappear later.

Professionals

While many network problems can be resolved with basic testing, there is no substitute for hiring trained and qualified professionals to install and test the network.

Most professionals can eliminate a network problem in a matter of minutes, while it may take a less experienced administrator days to fix the problem.

Cable Testers

Problems with cable, such as breaks in the cable, can be very difficult to locate. There are many types of devices that allow a network administrator to test cable that has already been installed. Some simple devices check the continuity of cable to determine if there is a break, while other devices help pinpoint the location of a break in cable.

Broadcasts

Many network interface cards come equipped with testing software. These allow the network administrator to broadcast information that can be detected by other similar network interface cards on the network. Broadcasts are a good way to test connections in a network.

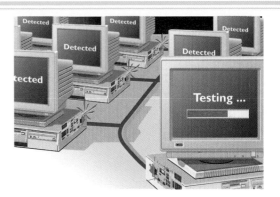

Traffic Simulators

Many network problems do not become apparent until the network is transferring a significant amount of information. Special devices and software programs are available that simulate traffic on a network similar to the amount that is generated when the network is in use.

CHAPTER 13

The Internet

The Internet is the world's largest computer network. This chapter explains the different components of the Internet, including the World Wide Web, Internet mail, Internet news and much more.

INTRODUCTION TO THE INTERNET

The Internet is the largest computer network in the world. Many company networks are connected to the Internet so they can use the valuable resources the Internet has to offer.

The Internet is often called the Net, the Information Superhighway or Cyberspace.

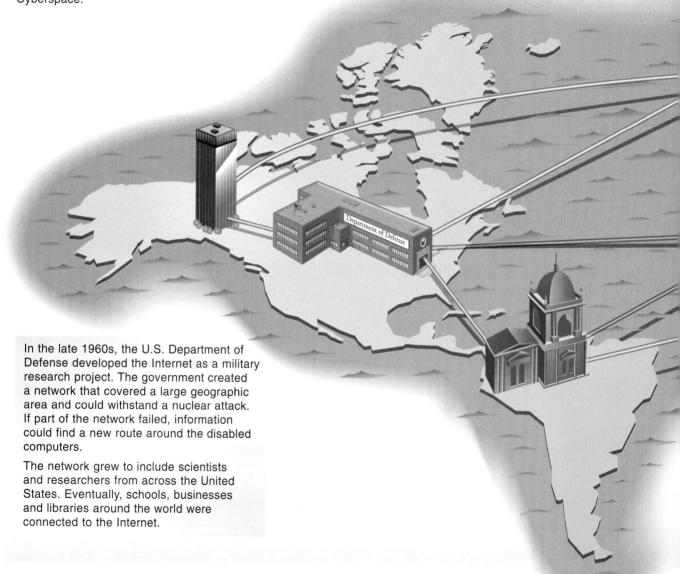

In the late 1960s, the U.S. Department of Defense developed the Internet as a military research project. The government created a network that covered a large geographic area and could withstand a nuclear attack. If part of the network failed, information could find a new route around the disabled computers.

The network grew to include scientists and researchers from across the United States. Eventually, schools, businesses and libraries around the world were connected to the Internet.

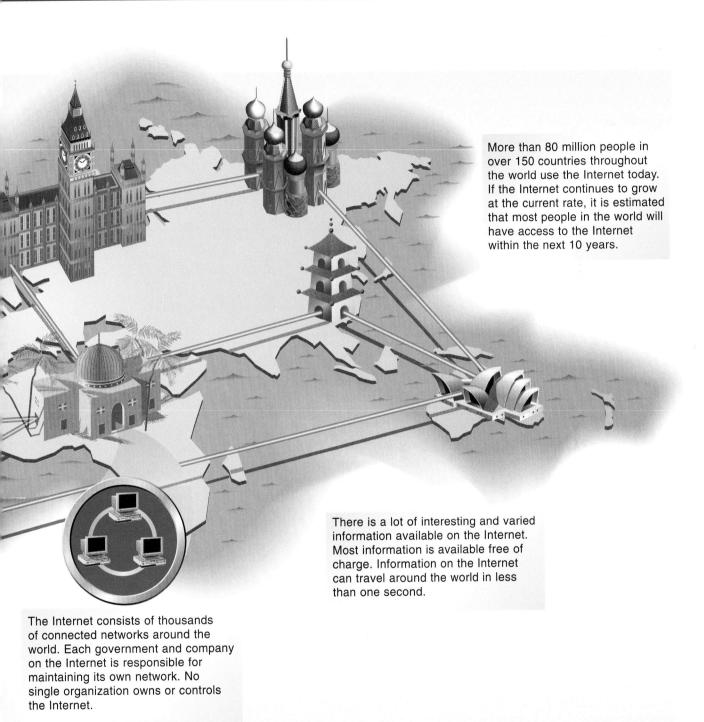

More than 80 million people in over 150 countries throughout the world use the Internet today. If the Internet continues to grow at the current rate, it is estimated that most people in the world will have access to the Internet within the next 10 years.

There is a lot of interesting and varied information available on the Internet. Most information is available free of charge. Information on the Internet can travel around the world in less than one second.

The Internet consists of thousands of connected networks around the world. Each government and company on the Internet is responsible for maintaining its own network. No single organization owns or controls the Internet.

THE WORLD WIDE WEB

The World Wide Web is one of the most widely used services available on the Internet today. The Web consists of a large collection of documents stored on computers around the world.

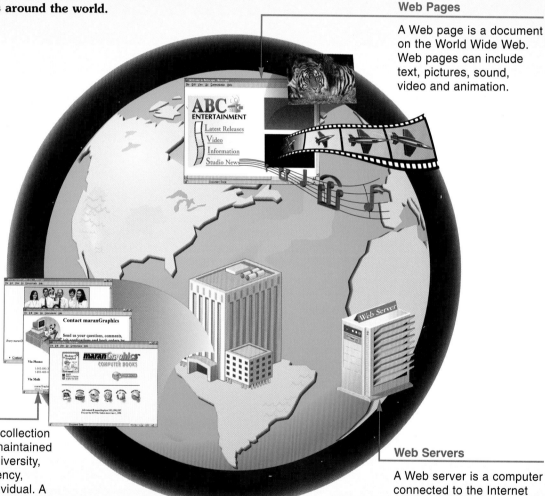

Web Pages

A Web page is a document on the World Wide Web. Web pages can include text, pictures, sound, video and animation.

Web Sites

A Web site is a collection of Web pages maintained by a college, university, government agency, company or individual. A Web site is an excellent way to promote a service or product to millions of people.

Web Servers

A Web server is a computer connected to the Internet that makes Web pages available to the world. A single server can store hundreds of Web sites.

Web Browsers

A Web browser is a software program that lets people view and explore sites on the World Wide Web.

Most Web browsers now incorporate features such as e-mail readers and news readers.

HTML

HyperText Markup Language (HTML) is used to create Web pages. HTML uses simple instructions, called tags, to display text and images in a Web page.

HTML tags are compact, allowing Web pages to transfer quickly over the Internet.

Creating Web Pages

Web pages are easy to create. Many programs are available that help users construct their own Web pages even if they are not familiar with HTML.

Many business software applications, such as word processors, can automatically transform documents into Web pages.

INTERNET MAIL

Connecting a network to the Internet allows users to exchange e-mail with people around the world. E-mail was one of the reasons the Internet was created.

E-mail Addresses

People must know the e-mail address of the person to whom they want to send a message. An e-mail address defines the location of an individual's mailbox on the Internet. An e-mail address consists of two parts separated by the @ (at) symbol.

The user name is the name of the person's account.

The domain name specifies the location of the person's account on the Internet.

Mail Servers

Each network that uses Internet e-mail has a mail server. A mail server is a computer responsible for handling all incoming and outgoing e-mail for the network.

When a message is addressed to jsmith@company.com, the mail server receives the message and then forwards it to the account called 'jsmith' on the network called 'company.com'.

E-mail Readers

An e-mail reader is a software program that allows people to send, receive and manage e-mail messages.

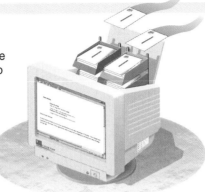

Many e-mail readers have advanced built-in features, such as automatic message sorting and spell checking.

Multimedia

Until recently, e-mail systems were used only to transfer text. It is now possible to exchange information such as pictures, sounds, videos and even software programs attached to e-mail messages.

E-mail Benefits

E-mail provides a fast and convenient way for users on a network to communicate with people all over the world. E-mail messages can travel around the world in seconds. Unlike telephone calls, e-mail messages do not require the recipient to be at the computer when the message arrives.

Using e-mail is also an inexpensive way to communicate. Once a network is connected to the Internet, there are no additional charges for exchanging e-mail.

Internet news allows people to post and read messages, called articles, on the Internet. Internet news, also known as Usenet (Users' Network), consists of many computers connected together to distribute articles.

comp.networks

biz.general

sci.med.pharmacy

Business News

Newsgroups

Newsgroups are the basis of Internet news. A newsgroup is a discussion group that allows people with common interests to discuss a particular topic. Newsgroups can be a great source of information regarding networking issues, such as security and administration.

alt.security

The name of a newsgroup describes the type of information discussed in the newsgroup. Most newsgroups do not monitor their articles, therefore some articles may contain unrelated topics.

News Readers

A news reader is a program that allows people to read and post articles to newsgroups. Many news readers offer features to help speed up and ease the process of reading and posting newsgroup articles.

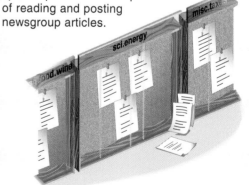

misc.taxes

sci.energy

food.wine

News readers can allow users to filter out unwanted articles, compose articles before connecting to the Internet and check the spelling in the articles before posting.

News Servers

A news server is a computer on the Internet that stores newsgroup articles. A user connects to a news server to post and read articles.

When a user posts an article to a newsgroup, the news server keeps a copy of the article and distributes it to other news servers around the world.

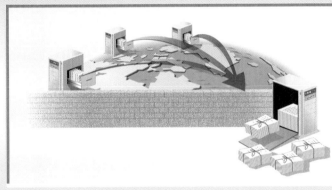

News Feeds

News servers exchange new newsgroup articles frequently to ensure every server has all of the available articles. The articles sent from one news server to another are referred to as a news feed. A news server may get news feeds from several different servers.

Binary Files

In addition to plain text, some newsgroup articles contain pictures and software programs. These pictures and programs are called binary files, or binaries. Most binaries posted in newsgroups are large and must be transmitted as a series of articles.

The articles must be decoded before the binary can be viewed or used. Some news readers automatically retrieve and decode all the articles that contain binary files.

Internet Relay Chat (IRC) is a system that allows users to instantly communicate with people around the world by typing messages back and forth.

IRC Networks

An IRC network is a group of IRC servers located all over the world that are connected to allow people to chat. There are many IRC networks. The largest network is called EFNet.

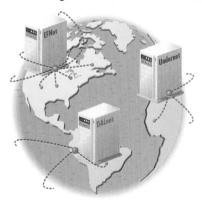

There can be well over 10,000 people using EFNet at any one time. Undernet and DALnet are smaller, yet popular, IRC networks. Smaller networks tend to be more reliable.

Channels

Each chat group, called a channel, usually focuses on a specific topic. A channel name often indicates the theme of the discussion.

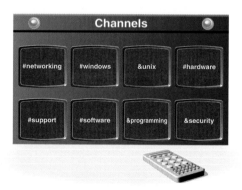

A # symbol in a channel name means the channel is available worldwide. An **&** symbol in a channel name means the channel is available only on the IRC server to which the user is connected.

IRC Programs

A user must have an IRC program to connect to an IRC server. Most IRC programs are easy to use and provide many features the user can customize. IRC programs allow users to connect to any IRC network and select from a large list of IRC servers.

Information

Although most people use IRC for social and informal chat, many IRC channels are used by people in related fields who can offer each other technical support. Most of these channels are network or computer oriented, such as #windows or #networking.

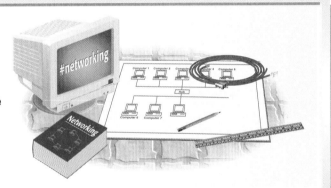

File Transfer

Most newer IRC programs allow users to transfer files to other people who are using IRC. Many people use this feature to exchange pictures or sound files. Transferring files using IRC can be slower than using other methods, such as FTP. Transferring large files using an IRC program is not recommended.

INTERNET FILE TRANSFER

File Transfer Protocol (FTP) is a system that allows users to transfer files to and from various computers on the Internet.

FTP Sites

An FTP site is a computer that stores files on the Internet. Colleges, universities, government agencies, companies and individuals maintain FTP sites.

There are thousands of FTP sites scattered across the Internet. Any type of file may be stored in an FTP site including text, images, sounds, videos and programs.

Private FTP Sites

Some FTP sites are private and require users to enter a password before accessing any files. Many corporations maintain private FTP sites to make files available to their employees and clients around the world.

Anonymous FTP Sites

Many FTP sites are anonymous. Anonymous FTP sites let users access files by entering their e-mail addresses instead of passwords. These sites store huge collections of files that anyone can download free of charge.

FTP Programs

An FTP program enables users to connect to FTP sites and transfer files. There are many FTP programs available. Most operating systems, such as Windows 95 and UNIX, already have basic FTP programs built in. Many Web browsers also have the ability to transfer files from FTP sites.

Transfer Type

Binary and ASCII are two file formats used to transfer files to and from an FTP site. Binary is best suited for transferring information such as software programs and compressed files. ASCII is often used for transferring text files. Most FTP programs can automatically choose the correct type of transfer file format.

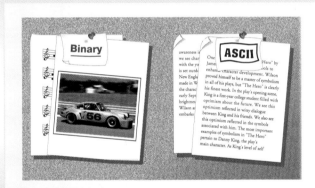

Transfer Speed

The speed at which files transfer to and from an FTP site can depend on the number of other users accessing the FTP site at the same time.

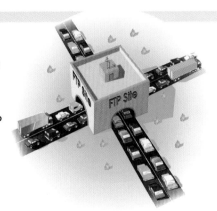

FTP sites that are maintained by companies and educational institutions are usually very busy during the day. Accessing these sites after business hours may result in faster transfer speeds.

People can use telnet to access information on another computer on the Internet.

Text-based

When people connect to another computer using telnet, lines of text appear without graphics. Users must type simple text commands to communicate with the other computer.

The computer often displays a list of options to choose from. The text may take a moment to appear on the screen, depending on the speed of the connection.

Telnet Programs

A telnet program is required to connect to another computer on the Internet. Most operating systems come equipped with basic telnet programs.

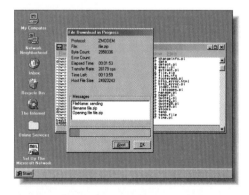

Many commercial telnet programs offer advanced features. Some telnet programs can even be used to transfer files.

Host Address

Before accessing a computer using telnet, a user must specify the name of the computer to which they want to connect. In most telnet programs, the user must type in the name of the computer, such as main.company.com

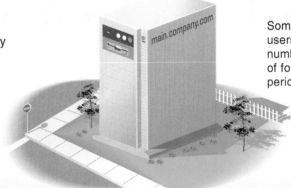

Some telnet programs require users to enter the computer's IP number. An IP number consists of four numbers separated by periods (.), such as 192.168.10.3

Information Services

Telnet is the easiest way for organizations to provide access to the information stored on mainframe computers or in large databases. Some government agencies and universities also make information available using telnet.

Troubleshooting

Network administrators can use telnet to troubleshoot problems with Internet servers.

For example, when a network administrator connects to a mail server using telnet, the administrator can determine whether there are any problems on the server.

CHAPTER 14

Connecting to the Internet

The Internet can be an invaluable addition to any network. This chapter discusses how to connect a network to the Internet and much more.

CONNECT A NETWORK TO INTERNET

Many companies are connecting their existing networks to the Internet. The Internet can be an invaluable tool for companies to provide and exchange information.

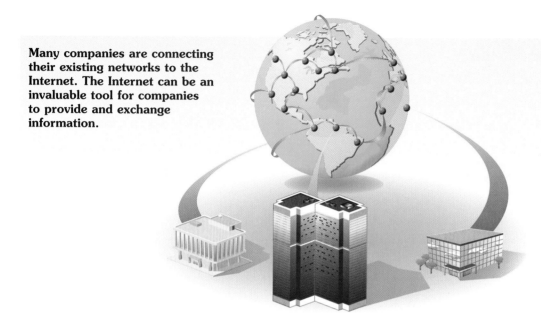

Purpose

Before connecting to the Internet, a company should determine what purpose a network connection to the Internet will serve.

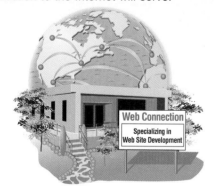

Many companies wish to have a Web site only to display information. In this case, a network connection to the Internet is unnecessary since a Web site can be created and implemented by a company that specializes in Web site development.

Planning

Before connecting a network to the Internet, a company should develop a detailed plan illustrating the exact process.

When connecting a network to the Internet, it will be necessary to purchase or lease costly equipment. Long-term contracts will also have to be made with companies, such as the local telephone company. Proper planning helps ensure that necessary services and equipment are used.

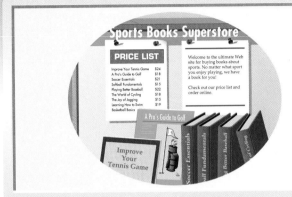

Provide Information

Companies use the Internet as a cost effective method of providing information to the public. Many companies use Web sites to provide information about the products and services they offer.

Access Information

The information available on the Internet is becoming better organized and easier to find. Most companies let their employees access the information available on the Internet. There are many databases and news services available, although a fee may be required to access some information.

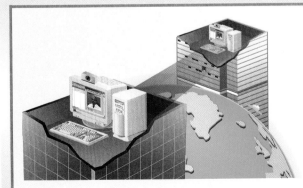

Communication

Companies can use the Internet to allow their employees to communicate using a variety of methods, such as e-mail or videoconferencing. The Internet can be an inexpensive method of communication between two companies in different locations, since telephone charges or postage fees do not apply. Companies also use the Internet as a way of communicating with their clients.

CONSIDERATIONS FOR CONNECTING TO INTERNET

There are many important aspects to consider when establishing and maintaining a connection between a company network and the Internet.

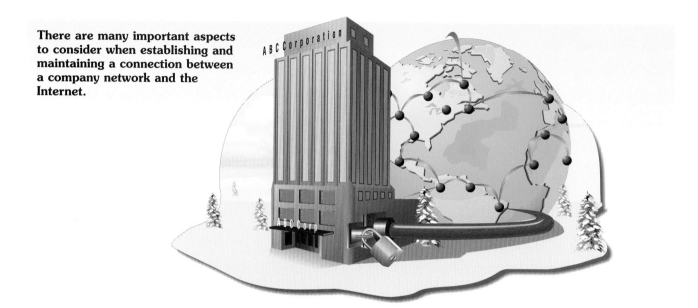

Training

When an existing network is connected to the Internet, many network users will have to be trained to work with the new applications used to access information.

Programs such as e-mail programs, Web browsers and file transfer programs can be very complex and users should know how to use them properly.

Support

Networks connected to the Internet require more support than other networks. If a company has a Web site, someone will have to create and maintain the Web pages stored on the Web site.

Personnel will also be required to support any new Internet-related hardware and software applications installed on the network.

Network Operating Systems

Many network operating system manufacturers make products that can simplify the process of connecting a network to the Internet. Before planning a connection to the Internet, the network administrator, or Internet service provider, should determine if there are any products that may help.

Backup

Companies that connect their networks to the Internet may rely heavily on the information and services available to them, such as e-mail. Some companies find it beneficial to have a second connection to the Internet using a different Internet service provider. Two connections to the Internet provide sufficient backup should one connection fail.

Security

Security concerns are an ongoing issue for network administrators. Security products and techniques are constantly evolving.

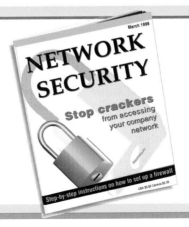

Network administrators who do not stay up-to-date with the latest security technologies risk a network attack from better-educated crackers.

CONSIDERATIONS FOR CONNECTING TO INTERNET

Budget

Planning, setting up and maintaining an Internet connection to a network can be very expensive.

Before a network administrator connects a network to the Internet, the necessary budget for a long-term connection should be determined.

Productivity

Many hours of productivity could be lost if employees use the Internet for non-work related tasks, such as personal Web browsing.

A network administrator should set and enforce rigid guidelines dictating how employees may use the Internet.

Reducing Costs

Connecting a network to the Internet often impacts on areas of a business that are not directly related to the use of the network.

By connecting their networks to the Internet, many companies reduce costs in areas such as long-distance telephone charges and research time.

HARDWARE CONSIDERATIONS

Connection Analysis

After a period of time, the network administrator should conduct a review of all the hardware and software components used to connect the network to the Internet.

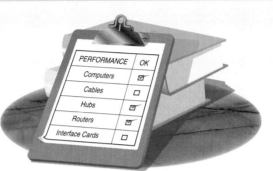

A thorough review of the connection can help the administrator determine the effectiveness of the connection.

Modem Sharing

New devices are now available that allow multiple modems to be used to provide a connection between a network and an Internet service provider.

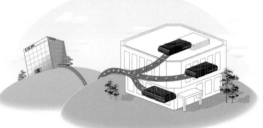

While these new devices may not be suitable for larger networks, they can be used on smaller networks that need to communicate with the Internet.

Scalable Hardware

Scalable hardware can be easily upgraded to adapt to new technologies. Hardware that is purchased to connect a network to the Internet should be scalable.

Since Internet technologies are constantly evolving, scalable hardware may help reduce the need to frequently purchase new hardware.

INTERNET SERVICE PROVIDERS

An Internet Service Provider (ISP) is a company that provides connections to the Internet for a fee. A network must connect to an Internet service provider in order to access the Internet.

Services

There are many Internet service providers offering a broad range of services. A company should carefully evaluate all aspects of an Internet service provider before deciding to use the services.

Contracts

Before using the services of an Internet service provider, a company typically has to enter into a contract, usually for a minimum of one year.

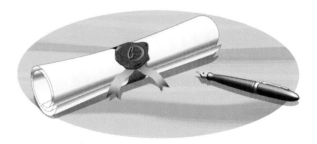

Every detail of the expected service should be written into the contract. This may help prevent unnecessary complications, such as the Internet service provider failing to provide acceptable levels of service. As with all contracts, a company should seek legal advice before committing to a long-term contract with an Internet service provider.

Size

An Internet service provider can be a relatively small business that provides Internet connections to companies, as well as dial-up services for home users. Many large Internet service providers connect businesses and organizations to the Internet using dedicated, high-speed connections.

Support and Equipment

Connecting a network to the Internet and maintaining a good quality connection is a technical process that requires trained personnel. The equipment used by an Internet service provider can determine the quality of a connection.

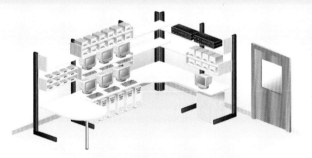

Companies should ensure an Internet service provider has the necessary personnel and equipment to properly support a connection to the Internet.

Network Access Points

Internet service providers exchange information with other Internet service providers at locations called Network Access Points (NAPs). Internet service providers connect to network access points using high-speed connections.

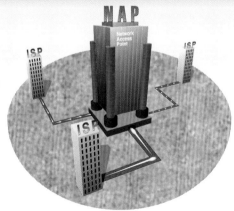

The faster a service provider's connection to a network access point, the faster a company's network connection to the Internet will be. Most Internet service providers can provide detailed information about their network speeds and traffic.

INTERNET HARDWARE

A variety of hardware
devices are required
when connecting a
network to the Internet.

Modems

Modems can be used to provide access between
a network and the Internet. A specialized software
application is often required to connect a network
to the Internet using a modem. Modems are slow
and allow a limited number of users access to the
Internet at a time. Modem access should only be
considered if a minimal amount of information will
be exchanged.

Routers

In most cases, routers connect a network to
the Internet. One router is connected to the
network while another router is connected to
the Internet service provider. The two routers
are joined by a dedicated connection. When
connected to the Internet by routers, the
network is considered part of the Internet and
users can access information immediately.

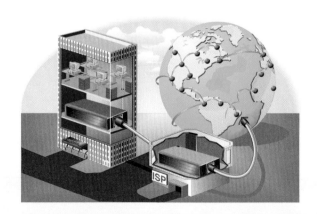

Firewalls

Security is a major consideration when connecting a network to the Internet. A firewall is a specialized computer that controls access to a network connected to the Internet.

Most devices that are used to connect networks to the Internet, such as routers, have basic firewall capabilities but may not provide enough protection for networks that contain confidential information.

Servers

Servers can be used to provide Internet services such as Web browsing, file access and e-mail capabilities to a network.

However, these servers may not be needed on a network as many Internet service providers offer these services.

Remote Access Servers

A company can use a remote access server to allow employees to connect to the Internet when away from the office.

For example, an employee can dial up, connect to the remote access server and then access the Internet through the company network. A remote access server typically consists of a computer connected to one or more modems.

INTERNET SOFTWARE

As well as computer hardware, a network may require software to connect to the Internet. Internet software may be required if a company wants to provide information on the Internet, or safeguard its own network information.

Connection Software

Establishing and maintaining a connection between a network and the Internet requires very little software. Most hardware that is used to connect networks to the Internet have built-in applications that allow the hardware to operate without the use of additional software.

Server Software

If a company wishes to set up and maintain its own Internet servers, such as Web servers, the network administrator will need to install the software required to run the Internet application. There are a number of server software programs available for free on the Internet. A company may also choose to purchase commercial software.

Application Software

Many networks connected to the Internet are starting to run applications that have been developed specifically for use on the Internet. Applications that make databases available on the Internet are becoming popular, as are applications that support credit card purchases.

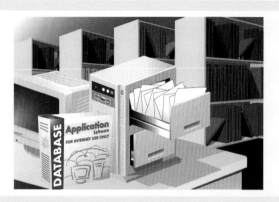

Security Software

Before a company can connect its network to the Internet, the network administrator may need to install software to monitor and prevent attacks from unauthorized users on the Internet.

Some types of security software can be installed on each network computer that accesses the Internet. Other types of security software can be installed on only one computer that is used to monitor and process all the information exchanged with the Internet.

Anti-virus Software

Many programs on the Internet contain viruses that may damage the information stored on a computer network. Anti-virus software should be installed on all computers that receive information from the Internet.

Some anti-virus software only need to be installed on one computer, which will examine all the information received from the Internet for viruses.

A high-speed connection is used to link a network with an Internet service provider.

The amount of information a connection to the Internet can transfer at once is referred to as bandwidth. The more bandwidth a company requires, the more expensive the connection to the Internet will be.

Installation

Proper planning is required for connecting a network to the Internet, since most connection types must be ordered weeks in advance of the required date. Most connection types require the local telephone company to install the connection.

Telephone Lines

Networks that do not exchange a lot of information with the Internet can use phone lines and modems to connect to the Internet. Modems can transfer information over phone lines at speeds of up to 33,600 bits per second (bps).

Some modems are capable of receiving information from the Internet at speeds of up to 56,000 bps, but can only send information at 33,600 bps.

HIGH-SPEED CONNECTIONS

ISDN

Integrated Services Digital Network (ISDN) is a connection that can be configured to exchange information at various speeds. The most common speed for connecting networks to the Internet is 128 kilobits per second (Kbps).

ISDN requires the use of special hardware on the network, such as ISDN routers or ISDN terminal adapters.

T1

T1 is a high-speed connection capable of transmitting information at 1.544 megabits per second (Mbps). Many small Internet service providers use a T1 connection to connect to the Internet.

If a company does not wish to pay for a full T1 line, the company may be able to use only part of the 1.544 Mbps capacity. This type of connection is referred to as a fractional T1.

T3

T3 is a connection capable of transmitting information over fiber-optic cable at speeds of up to 44.73 Mbps. T3 connections are often used to connect large Internet service providers to the Internet.

Only large companies that exchange large amounts of information with the Internet use T3 connections.

Any computer or network that exchanges information with the Internet must use the TCP/IP protocol suite. Configuring a network connection to an Internet service provider using TCP/IP protocols can be a very complex and time-consuming operation.

IP Addresses

Before using TCP/IP to connect a network to the Internet, each computer that accesses the Internet will have to get a unique IP address. IP addresses are written as four numbers separated by dots, such as 192.168.67.54. This is known as dotted decimal notation.

Getting an IP Address

An Internet service provider obtains the required IP numbers from a central organization called the Internet Network Information Center (InterNIC). Because each IP address must be unique, the Internet is running out of IP addresses. A new system of IP addressing, called IPv6, will provide more IP numbers in the future.

Assigning IP Numbers

There are two ways to assign IP numbers to computers on a network. One way is to configure each computer separately so it will always use the same IP number. Another way is to set up a dedicated server, called a BOOTP or DHCP server, to assign IP numbers to computers automatically. The type of server used depends on which TCP/IP protocol is used to assign the IP numbers.

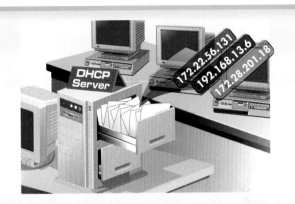

DNS Servers

DNS servers are used to convert IP addresses into readable names, such as www.company.com. When connecting a network to the Internet, the Internet service provider's DNS servers are often used. If many computers on a network access the Internet, the network may have its own DNS server.

Drivers

Before a computer can access the Internet, it must have the TCP/IP protocol suite and the appropriate TCP/IP drivers installed. The TCP/IP drivers convert information from the computer into information that can be transferred on a TCP/IP network.

TROUBLESHOOT INTERNET CONNECTIONS

There are many problems that can occur when a network is connected to the Internet. For most companies, it is essential that the network administrator be able to quickly locate and fix Internet connection problems.

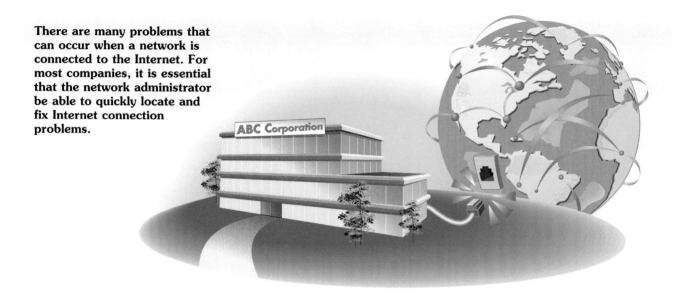

Notes

Keeping detailed notes and logs about connection problems is vital. Many network connection problems are simply symptoms of larger problems. Detailed notes and connection diagrams can help network administrators and service personnel quickly track down the source of a problem.

Hardware

Many hardware products are now available that can alert the network administrator when a problem is detected. Complex networking components often use methods such as e-mail or paging to alert a network administrator when an error occurs, such as a broken connection. Some simple hardware devices use colored lights to indicate that an error has occurred.

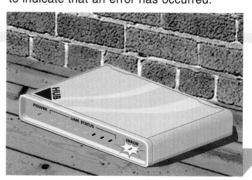

PING

PING is a very simple utility that is available on most computers using the TCP/IP protocol suite. The PING program sends information to a computer on a network and then reports how long it takes to receive a reply from the destination computer. PING is an invaluable tool for establishing whether a connection between two computers has been broken.

TCP/IP Protocol Analyzers

If there are any difficulties with an Internet connection, a protocol analyzer can be used to examine the traffic on the connection and pinpoint the problem. For example, a TCP/IP protocol analyzer can be used to examine each piece of data transferred over the connection to determine whether the data contains any errors.

Support

Most Internet service providers now offer very good technical support. Some Internet service providers offer 24-hour support over the phone. The Internet service provider's support team should be available to help the network administrator troubleshoot any Internet connection problems.

Intranets

An intranet is a network, similar to the Internet, within a company. This chapter discusses some of the features available on intranets, including videoconferencing, e-mail, newsgroups and much more.

INTRODUCTION TO INTRANETS

An intranet is a network, similar to the Internet, within a company or organization. Intranets offer many of the features and services available on the Internet such as Web systems, e-mail, newsgroups and chat.

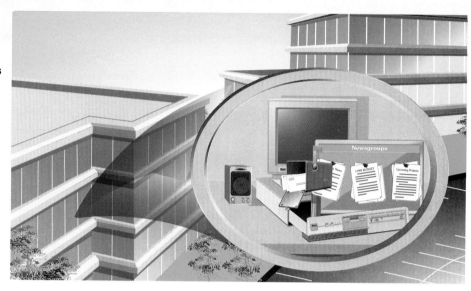

Efficiency

Intranets allow employees of a company to access information quickly and efficiently. When information is easy to access, it often increases the productivity of a company.

For example, employees can access a phone directory on the intranet instead of contacting the receptionist for numbers.

Servers

Intranets use special computers called servers to control the distribution of information on an intranet.

On most intranets, one server is connected to the network for each intranet feature required, such as an e-mail or Web system. Many intranet servers are similar to the servers used on the Internet.

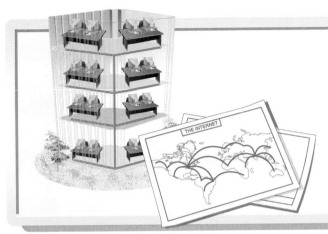

Internet Technology

Intranets transfer information on a network using the same technology that is used to transfer information on the Internet. This allows intranets to exchange information quickly and easily over different types of networks, without having to consider the network operating systems used on each network.

User Control

Many software programs allow users on an intranet to provide information from their own computers to other users on the intranet. For example, before going on vacation, a user could create a personal Web page for others to read. Information on the page could include emergency contacts and the days the user will be absent.

Software

The software used to exchange information on an intranet, such as a Web browser or e-mail reader, is the same as the software used to exchange information on the Internet. Most required software is available at computer stores or on the Internet.

VIDEOCONFERENCING ON INTRANETS

Videoconferencing can make communication more efficient. By using their computers, people on an intranet can see and hear each other when they are communicating. Videoconferencing is just starting to become feasible on intranets.

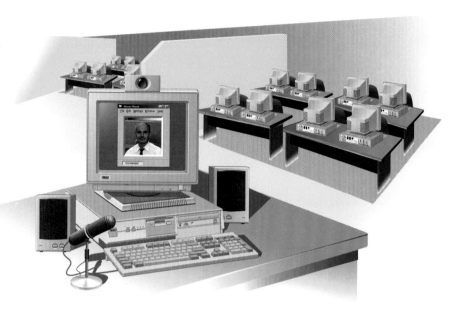

Face to Face

Videoconferencing allows people to have face-to-face conversations with other users on an intranet, whether they are around the corner or on the other side of the city.

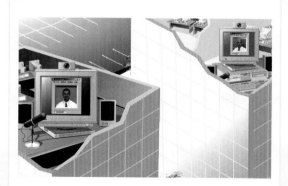

Videoconferencing transmits audio and video signals over the intranet, which allows users to communicate with each other.

Multiple Participants

One of the most promising aspects of videoconferencing on intranets is the ability to have several people participate in a videoconference at once. Although videoconferencing is still not feasible for large groups, it is possible to effectively videoconference with up to three other people.

Time-consuming tasks, such as meetings in person, may eventually be replaced by videoconferencing.

Bandwidth

Videoconferencing requires a lot of information to transfer between computers. Many existing networks are not capable of transmitting information fast enough to support a large number of videoconferencing computers.

If the bandwidth on a network is not sufficient to host a videoconference, all users of the network may be affected.

Equipment

Specific equipment is required for videoconferencing. A computer must have a sound card with speakers and a microphone attached to transmit and receive sound.

The computer must also have a video camera attached to transmit video images.

Training

Videoconferencing can be a useful tool for providing training to a new employee located in another office.

Using videoconferencing, a member of the training team can provide audio and visual guidance to another person without actually being at the same location. This may substantially reduce travel and training costs for a company.

SCHEDULING ON INTRANETS

The ability to organize and schedule meetings and projects is one of the most important services available on an intranet.

JUNE 1998

Electronic Diaries

Most people use some kind of diary to remind them of appointments, keep notes and store the names and phone numbers of their contacts. Some electronic diaries, or scheduling programs, can be used on an intranet to coordinate the activities of groups of people.

Schedule Meetings

Planning and organizing meetings can be a time-consuming task since everyone in a company may have a different agenda. Scheduling meetings for large groups of people on an intranet can be made much easier by using scheduling software.

Scheduling software may be used to check employee availability and to schedule meetings at a time and place convenient for everyone.

Schedule Resources

A resource can be an object such as a printer, or a person such as a consultant, needed for the completion of a project. Scheduling software can be used to manage and schedule the use of resources to ensure they are available when required.

The time and expense of a project can be better managed by properly scheduling the use of resources.

Monitor Resources

One of the benefits of using scheduling software is that users can monitor how a company's resources are used.

Problems, such as a resource shortage, may be avoided before they occur because users can track how often people use a given resource.

Automatic Scheduling

Some scheduling software can perform tasks such as booking a boardroom automatically when a user requests a meeting.

When a user requests a meeting, the scheduling software can also send an automatic invitation to everyone who needs to attend the meeting. The time and place of the meeting will be added to each person's schedule.

INTRANET WEB SYSTEMS

Sites on an intranet Web system are similar to Web sites found on the World Wide Web.

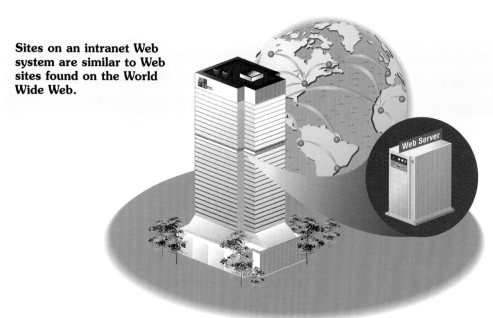

Web servers connected to a network store the Web sites and manage the intranet Web system.

Compatibility

Intranets are very useful for companies that have different types of computers, such as Macintosh and IBM-compatible. Any computer on the intranet that can run a Web browser can access the information available on the intranet Web system.

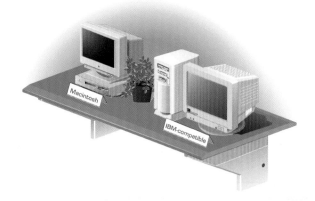

Privacy

Many documents found on an intranet, such as company policies or sales reports, are not made available to the general public.

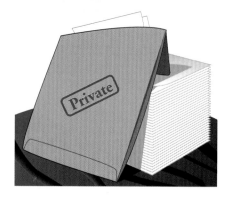

A company's intranet Web server is different from the Web server the company uses to provide information on the Internet. This ensures that information on the intranet Web system is not accessible from the Internet.

Employee Web Pages

If employees are connected to an intranet, they can easily publish their own intranet Web pages. Web pages can contain information such as office telephone numbers, current projects or any other information that might be important to fellow employees.

Department Web Pages

If a company has an intranet, any department in the company can display information on its own set of intranet Web pages.

The human resources department may display company policies and schedules. The sales department might publish Web pages providing the latest sales figures.

Create Web Pages

Many applications are now capable of converting documents into Web pages. Most word processors, spreadsheets and database programs have a feature that makes it possible to save documents in the HTML format.

The documents can then be transferred to a Web site on the intranet.

E-MAIL ON INTRANETS

Many company networks use e-mail systems that only allow employees to exchange simple text. Intranets allow companies to exchange messages using the same type of e-mail systems found on the Internet.

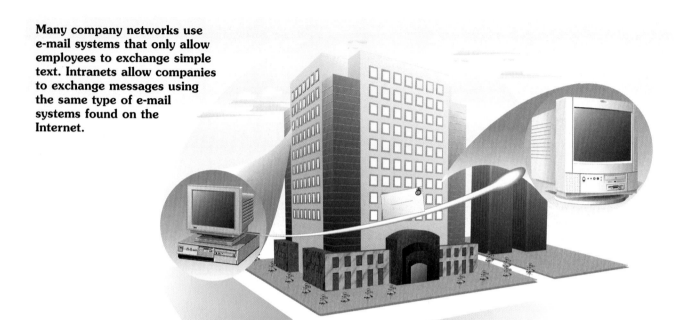

E-mail Features

E-mail is one of the first Internet technologies to become widely used on intranets. While basic e-mail systems exist in some network operating systems, Internet-like e-mail offers a wider variety of features to intranet users.

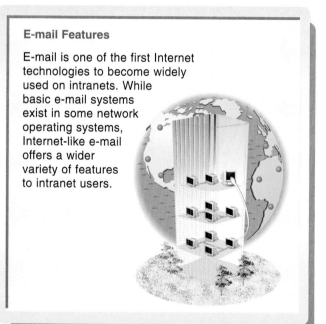

Multimedia

Users can send a wide variety of information using e-mail on an intranet. Almost any type of file can be attached to an e-mail message, making e-mail systems an efficient way of distributing files such as images, word processing documents or spreadsheets.

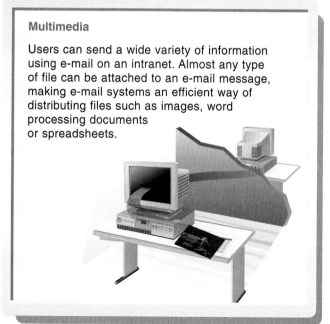

Multiple Recipients

Sending the same e-mail message to several people at once is a quick and effective method for distributing information on an intranet.

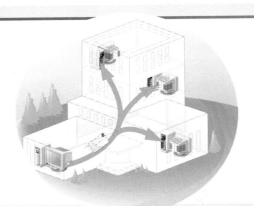

Many companies store the intranet e-mail addresses of every user in a single address book that can be accessed by everyone on the intranet.

Message Filters

People on intranets often receive many e-mail messages every hour. To help organize messages, filters are now being included with e-mail readers. Filters allow the user to sort e-mail messages according to various criteria, such as the sender or subject of the message.

Internet Access

If the company network is connected to the Internet, users of the intranet can also use the intranet e-mail reader to exchange messages with people on the Internet.

NEWSGROUPS ON INTRANETS

Many company intranets use newsgroups that are similar to the newsgroups found on the Internet.

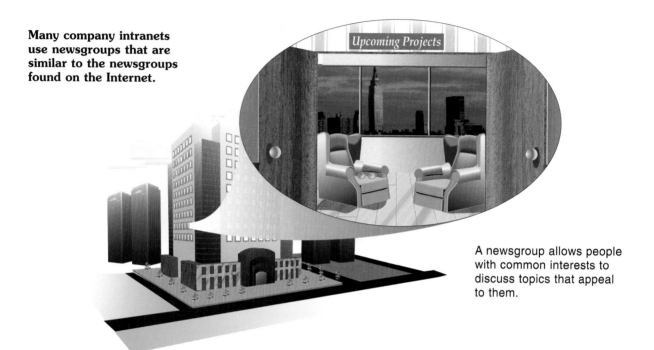

A newsgroup allows people with common interests to discuss topics that appeal to them.

Read-only Newsgroups

Many companies use newsgroups to provide information such as announcements, sales figures or general company information.

Each employee can access these newsgroups and read the posted information. Employees are usually not allowed to post messages to these types of newsgroups.

Project Newsgroups

Within any large organization there are teams of people who work together on different projects. If a company provides newsgroups on its intranet, the company can create a newsgroup for each project.

This will allow members of a team working on the same project to conveniently exchange ideas and information.

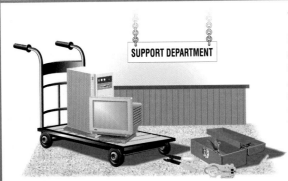

Technical Support Newsgroups

Most large companies have a technical support department dedicated to installing and maintaining their computer systems. A company may want to have a technical support newsgroup where users can post questions and read answers or suggestions from the support department.

Customized Newsgroups

In addition to creating their own newsgroups, companies can also purchase other types of information in the form of newsgroup messages, called articles. For example, a stock brokerage may purchase the latest news from stock markets around the world to display on its intranet.

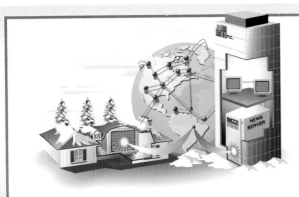

Customer Access

Many companies are now making their private intranet newsgroups available to their customers and clients on the Internet. Providing Internet access to a company's intranet news server allows people to ask questions about a product or service, provide feedback to the company and communicate with other customers.

CHAT ON INTRANETS

Companies can set up chat channels on an intranet like the ones found on the Internet Relay Chat (IRC) system.

Chatting

People using an intranet chat system can instantly communicate with one or more users on the intranet. When a user types text, the text appears on the screen of each person involved in the conversation. The name of the person who typed the text appears in front of the text.

Channels

An intranet chat system may have multiple channels, with each channel dedicated to the discussion of a single topic. Chat channels are often used to allow employees in different locations to efficiently discuss team projects. The name of a channel usually indicates the topic of discussion. For example, a channel called Marketing may be started to discuss current marketing strategies and projects.

Multimedia

Most chat systems let people send and receive files with others who are chatting in the same channel on the intranet. Many intranet chat systems are very elaborate and allow people to exchange more than just text files.

Some chat systems also allow users to display images or play sounds for other people in the same channel.

Technical Support

Many companies are now using chat systems to provide technical support to their employees.

Technical support people make themselves available for chatting so employees can ask questions and instantly get answers.

Logs

Each user can save the text displayed in a chat channel as a file called a log. Chat logs can be useful if the chat channel is being used to exchange technical or detailed information. This lets users keep a record of the information that is discussed while chatting.

Chat logs can also be used to save any information that may have been displayed while a user was away from the computer.

FILE TRANSFER ON INTRANETS

File sharing is one of the main reasons a company would set up an intranet.

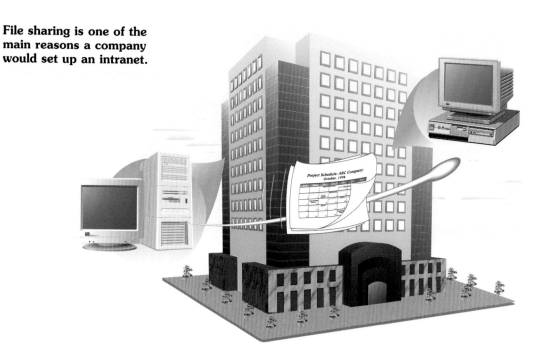

File Transfer Protocol

File transfer on an intranet can be achieved using the File Transfer Protocol (FTP) system. Using FTP to transfer files allows computers running different operating systems, such as Macintosh and Windows, to access the same files. A Web browser is often the only program required to access files using FTP.

Internet Access

If the company network is connected to the Internet, the company intranet can be used to transfer files to the Internet. For example, instead of using floppy disks and a delivery service to send files to a professional printer, a company can use FTP to transfer the files to the printer over the Internet.

Transfer Speed

Network technology is capable of transferring information at much higher speeds than the Internet. Intranets can transfer information at these high speeds because they use a company's existing network. The faster speed also makes intranets an effective network alternative for transferring large files that would take a long time to transfer on the Internet.

Access Information

The ability to efficiently access information in a company is essential. Many companies store frequently accessed documents on an FTP server on the intranet. Many types of files, such as word-processing, spreadsheet and graphics files, can all be quickly accessed from an FTP server.

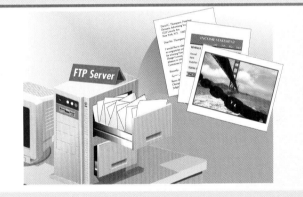

Program Updates

The high speed of information transfer on an intranet makes it possible to quickly transfer large programs. New software products and software upgrades can be transferred to a computer using an intranet.

INTRANET SOFTWARE

A company must have
intranet software to
set up an intranet.
There are many types
of intranet software
available.

Free Software

Software available for the Internet, such as
Web browsers, e-mail and news readers, FTP
programs and chat software, can also be used
on a corporate intranet.

Many of these software programs are
available on the Internet for a low fee
or free of charge.

Intranet Suites

An intranet suite is a collection of several different
applications sold together in one package. Intranet
suites usually consist of e-mail, Web publishing,
database and security applications.

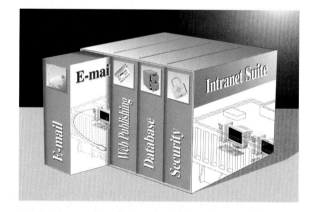

When installing an intranet suite, a network
administrator can decide which applications
to use and install only those required.

POPULAR INTRANET SUITES

Lotus Domino

IBM offers the Lotus Domino intranet software suite, formerly known as Lotus Notes. Domino provides many standard features that make it easy to communicate and share information on an intranet.

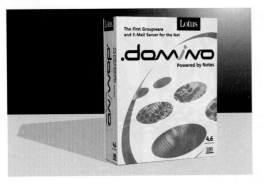

Microsoft BackOffice

Microsoft offers a set of intranet software called BackOffice. BackOffice also includes an application called FrontPage that helps users easily organize and manage a large Web site.

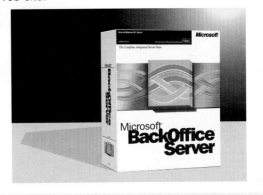

Netscape SuiteSpot

The company that created the Navigator Web browser also offers intranet software in a package called SuiteSpot. SuiteSpot is a collection of software that provides many popular intranet features.

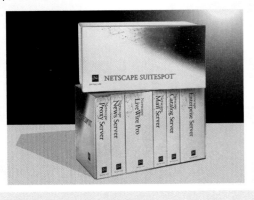

Novell IntranetWare

Novell is well known for its NetWare networking software and also offers intranet software, called IntranetWare. IntranetWare offers many basic intranet features, but the main advantage of the suite is its compatibility with the Novell networking software.

GROUPWARE

Groupware is software that allows users to work together in groups on a network or intranet.

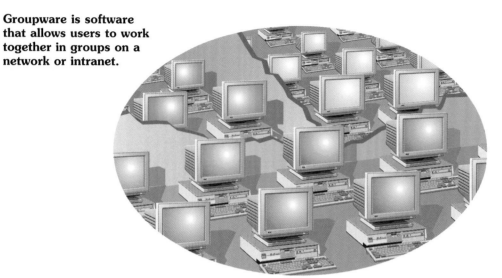

Groupware products and intranets are gradually merging because both let users access and use information on a network in a more productive manner.

Groups

In an organization or business, work is often completed by groups or teams. Most employees belong to at least one group.

Groupware is used to track the activities of groups and is particularly useful for organizing the activities of large groups.

Collaboration

Groupware products allow people in a group to easily work together on projects. For example, when using groupware to collaborate on a document, all group members can make changes, review changes made by other members or refer to earlier versions of the document.

This type of collaboration enables groups to accomplish tasks and projects efficiently.

Communication

One of the most important features of groupware is its ability to allow group members to easily and efficiently communicate with each other.

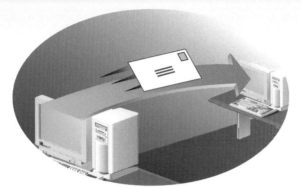

Most groupware products include an electronic mail (e-mail) feature.

Information Flow

A difficult aspect of business is monitoring and organizing the circulation of information within a company, commonly referred to as the paper trail.

PAPER TRAIL
Document Name: Proposal for New Product Line

To:	From:	Comments	Authorization	Time
Human Resources	Management	Number of new employees needed for project	S. Kates	10:06 AM
Accounting	Human Resources	Cost analysis needed	J. Humphrey	11:02 AM
Sales	Accounting	Comments	H. Peterson	1:30 PM
Marketing	Sales	Comments	P. Smith	2:45 PM

Groupware is used to track the flow of information and to help determine if any changes should be made for improvement.

Tracking

Groupware can be used to monitor, track and schedule the various stages of a project.

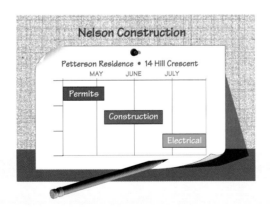

As well as tracking the project, groupware can be used to forecast future resource requirements, such as equipment or consultants.

INDEX

INDEX

INDEX

INDEX

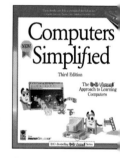

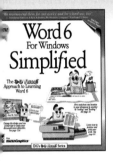

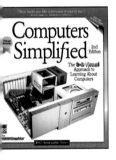

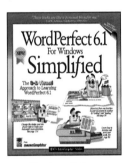
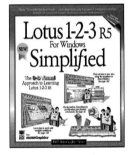

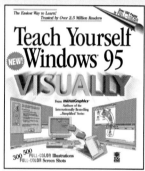

ORDER FORM

TRADE & INDIVIDUAL ORDERS

Phone: **(800) 762-2974**
or **(317) 895-5200**
(8 a.m.–6 p.m., CST, weekdays)
FAX : **(317) 895-5298**

EDUCATIONAL ORDERS & DISCOUNTS

Phone: **(800) 434-2086**
(8:30 a.m.–5:00 p.m., CST, weekdays)
FAX : **(817) 251-8174**

CORPORATE ORDERS FOR 3-D VISUAL™ SERIES

Phone: **(800) 469-6616**
(8 a.m.–5 p.m., EST, weekdays)
FAX : **(905) 890-9434**

Qty	ISBN	Title	Price	Total

Shipping & Handling Charges

	Description	First book	Each add'l. book	Total
Domestic	Normal	$4.50	$1.50	$
	Two Day Air	$8.50	$2.50	$
	Overnight	$18.00	$3.00	$
International	Surface	$8.00	$8.00	$
	Airmail	$16.00	$16.00	$
	DHL Air	$17.00	$17.00	$

Subtotal _____

CA residents add
applicable sales tax _____

IN, MA and MD
residents add
5% sales tax _____

IL residents add
6.25% sales tax _____

RI residents add
7% sales tax _____

TX residents add
8.25% sales tax _____

Shipping _____

Total _____

Ship to:

Name_____

Address_____

Company_____

City/State/Zip_____

Daytime Phone_____

Payment: ☐ Check to IDG Books (US Funds Only)

☐ Visa ☐ Mastercard ☐ American Express

Card # _____ Exp. _____ Signature_____

maranGraphics™